for Maggie
whose idea inspired this book

Location of Walks
Berwick
River Tweed
Norham
Walk 10
A1
Beal
Walk 9
Holy Island
Coldstream
Etal
Lowick
Crookham
Ford
Walk 8
Walk 7
Holburn
Bamburgh
Belford
Doddington
Walk 5
A697
Seahouses
Kirknewton
Akeld
River Till
Walk 6
Wooler
Chatton
Walk 4
A697
A1
Embleton
Walk 3
Eglingham
Cheviot Hills
Powburn
Ingram
River Aln
Glanton
Alnwick
Walk 2
Alnmouth
Alnham
A697
Netherton
Alwinton
A1
Amble
River Coquet
Walk 1
Longframlington
Rothbury
Felton
A68
A697
Otterburn

Contents

Introduction

This book describes ten circular walks that offer local people and visitors the opportunity to explore and enjoy that beautiful, but often forgotten, part of north Northumberland that lies sandwiched between the Cheviot Hills and the Northumberland Coast. The routes vary in length from about 4 to 6 miles and most can be completed, with relative ease, in about half a day or less, even by relatively inexperienced walkers. All of the walks follow tracks and paths that take you through some of Northumberland's most unspoilt landscapes which have a fascinating and unique history and heritage as well as a wonderful sense of peace and tranquillity.

Thousands of years ago this land was occupied by ancient Britons who eked out a living by growing crops and raising liverstock: evidence of their passing can still be seen in the remains of the hillforts and settlements that are scattered across the landscape. In later centuries the Romans came and went but, during the 'Dark Ages' that followed, the kingdom of Northumbria, stretching from the River Humber to the Lothians, became a major seat of power and a centre for Christian learning and culture. The Lindisfarne Gospels, which date from this period, remain one of the world's outstanding early Christian achievements. In the mediaeval period this border country formed the backdrop to many battles that shaped the future of both England and Scotland. During these lawless times, local farms and villages were at the mercy of marauding bands of Border Reivers and life was hard and sometimes short. With the coming of peace, people fell into a more settled pattern of existence and agriculture became the lifeblood of the area, although nowadays tourism plays an increasingly important role in the economic survival of its rural communities.

The walks in this book have been chosen to help you enjoy and learn about this area's rich and colourful history and the interpretive notes that have been included for each walk focus on this historical and archaeological theme, although you will also find lots of information about the local landscape, geology and wildlife. Walking can be thirsty and hungry work so the introduction to each walk gives the location of nearby restaurants and cafés, pubs and shops which we hope you will support during your visit.

Walk Routes

The book is aimed at anyone who wants to spend a few hours enjoying a pleasant and interesting walk, with the opportunity for a pub lunch, afternoon tea or an ice cream to finish off. At the start of each walk there is a brief introduction to give you a flavour of the route that you will take. This is followed by a note of the 1:25000 OS Explorer Map for the walk and the six figure grid reference for the start; an indication of its degree of difficulty (easy, moderate or strenuous); its length and the time that it should take to complete (allowing for a few stops along the way); and the height and gradient of any uphill sections. To help you get the most out of your walk and learn something about the area's history, culture and wildlife, lots of information is included about points of interest along the way.

The walks mostly follow designated public footpaths and bridleways: these are normally signposted (with timber finger posts) only where they leave a public highway. Waymarkers may have been installed at other locations (e.g. on a stile or at a gateway) where the alignment of a right of way is unclear. In some cases the walks cross 'access land' where you have a 'right to roam' (see below for details). On a couple of occasions the walk route has been provided by the landowner or is used with their consent: in these cases the routes are marked on the maps as 'permissive access' (see page 6 for map key).

Access Land and the 'Right to Roam'

Much of the open hill land in north Northumberland is defined as 'access land' (under the terms of the Countryside and Rights of Way Act 2000) where the public has a 'right to roam' wherever they want – but only on foot, not by cycle or on a horse. These areas are clearly signed at both entry and exit points (see examples below) and are also shown on the new editions of the Ordnance Survey 'Explorer Maps' (1: 25000) although it is important to be aware that restrictions to this right of access may apply at certain times of year or in certain locations: so please be sure to comply with any notices that may have been posted.

Maps

The start point for each of the ten walks is shown on the location map on page 2. The individual maps for each walk have been drawn specially for this book and are carefully cross referenced to the route descriptions in the text with the aim of making it as simple as possible for you to find your way. Alongside information about the nature of the route, reference is made to different structures such as gates, stiles, finger posts and waymarkers that you will encounter along the way. The walks in this book are covered by the following OS maps:

- 1:25000 Outdoor Leisure Map OL16 (The Cheviot Hills): Walks 2 & 6
- 1:25000 Explorer Map 332 (Alnwick and Amble): Walks 1 & 3
- 1:25000 Explorer Map 339 (Kelso & Lower Tweed Valley): Walks 8 & 10
- 1:25000 Explorer Map 340 (Holy Island and Bamburgh): Walks 4, 5, 7 & 9

Key

	walk route (with right of access)	G	field gate/wicket gate
	walk route (permissive access)	S	stile
	road	CG	cattle grid
	track	F	finger post
	other path (not part of walk)	W	waymarker
i	information centre	P	car park

Looking after the Countryside

Most of the land along these walks is privately owned. It is in everyone's interest to look after the countryside and to leave it as they would like to find it. In particular, fasten all gates and keep to the recognised route, especially when crossing enclosed farmland. It is also important to act responsibly and considerately by keeping to the Country Code - so take any litter home, don't disturb livestock and, if you wish to take a dog, keep it on a lead at all times.

Safety Advice

All of these walks are along paths and tracks across open countryside and there are a number of points that should be borne in mind, especially if you are taking young children.

Weather & Clothing

Comfort is essential to the enjoyment of any walk so wear comfortable, sensible shoes or boots. From May to October conditions underfoot will usually be fairly good, although at other times of the year or after heavy rain the ground may be soft and boggy in places. Walking can also be warm work but, especially at higher levels, it is possible to become chilled so take an extra layer of clothing just in case the temperature drops.

Even in summer, rain clouds can sweep in remarkably quickly and, in the best traditions of the British climate, what promises to be a warm, clear and sunny day can soon turn out to be cool, wet and windy. So, however good the weather forecast, always take a waterproof, remembering that it can keep out the wind as well as the rain.

Hopefully you will experience none of these more unsavoury elements of the British weather and you will enjoy your walk on a fine day with blue skies. At such times, you can get thirsty and the sun can be strong - so go prepared with a hat, sun cream and plenty to drink.

Hazards

Some of the walks include steep ascents and descents: these may be grassy, rocky or have a loose stony surface. Take great care, especially if the ground is wet and slippery, remembering that more accidents happen going downhill than uphill. On Walk 9, the section to the west of Nessend runs along the top of a high sea cliff: please take extreme care here, especially if it is windy or wet, if you are accompanied by children or dogs, or if you suffer from vertigo. Some walks also include sections along minor roads. Although many of these roads are likely to be relatively quiet, walkers should, wherever possible, use the pavement or verge. If you have to walk on the road, keep to the right hand side so that you face oncoming vehicles and be sure to watch and listen for approaching traffic.

Mobile Phones

A mobile phone can be a God-send in an emergency but remember that out of towns coverage can be patchy and you may not be able to get through - so don't rely on your mobile to get you out of trouble.

1. Lord Armstrong's Rothbury Carriage Drive

STARTING FROM JUST OUTSIDE THE MARKET TOWN OF ROTHBURY, this walk follows the route of a 19th century carriage drive around the southern edge of Cartington Moor. The drive was designed by Lord Armstrong so that his family and friends could enjoy the attractive scenery of the Cragside Estate: a century later, the landscape has lost none of its charm and beauty, with distant views to the west along the River Coquet and north to the Cheviot Hills.

OS Map:	*1:25000 Explorer Map 332 (Alnwick and Amble)*
Start:	*NU 067033*
Grade:	*Easy, with a good surface for most of the route and few climbs*
Length:	*5.3 miles (8.5 km) and about 3 hours*
Ascent:	*170 metres (550 feet) on gentle gradients*

Local services
- Rothbury & Longframlington
- Rothbury, Thropton, Forest Burn Gate, Weldon Bridge
- Rothbury, Thropton & Longframlington

Drive out of Rothbury on the Alnwick road (B6341). After about 1¼ miles you will pass the entrance to 'Cragside: House and Estate' (a National Trust property that is well worth a visit). Half a mile further on, turn left into the Forestry Commission's 'Debdon' wood: there is a very distinctive sign at the entrance. (Note that this sign is not visible if you are travelling from the Alnwick direction towards Rothbury). Just inside the entrance, park in the open area on the right hand side of the track. PLEASE TAKE CARE NOT TO BLOCK THE FORESTRY COMMISSION BARRIER.

Primrose Cottage and south west towards Ship Crag

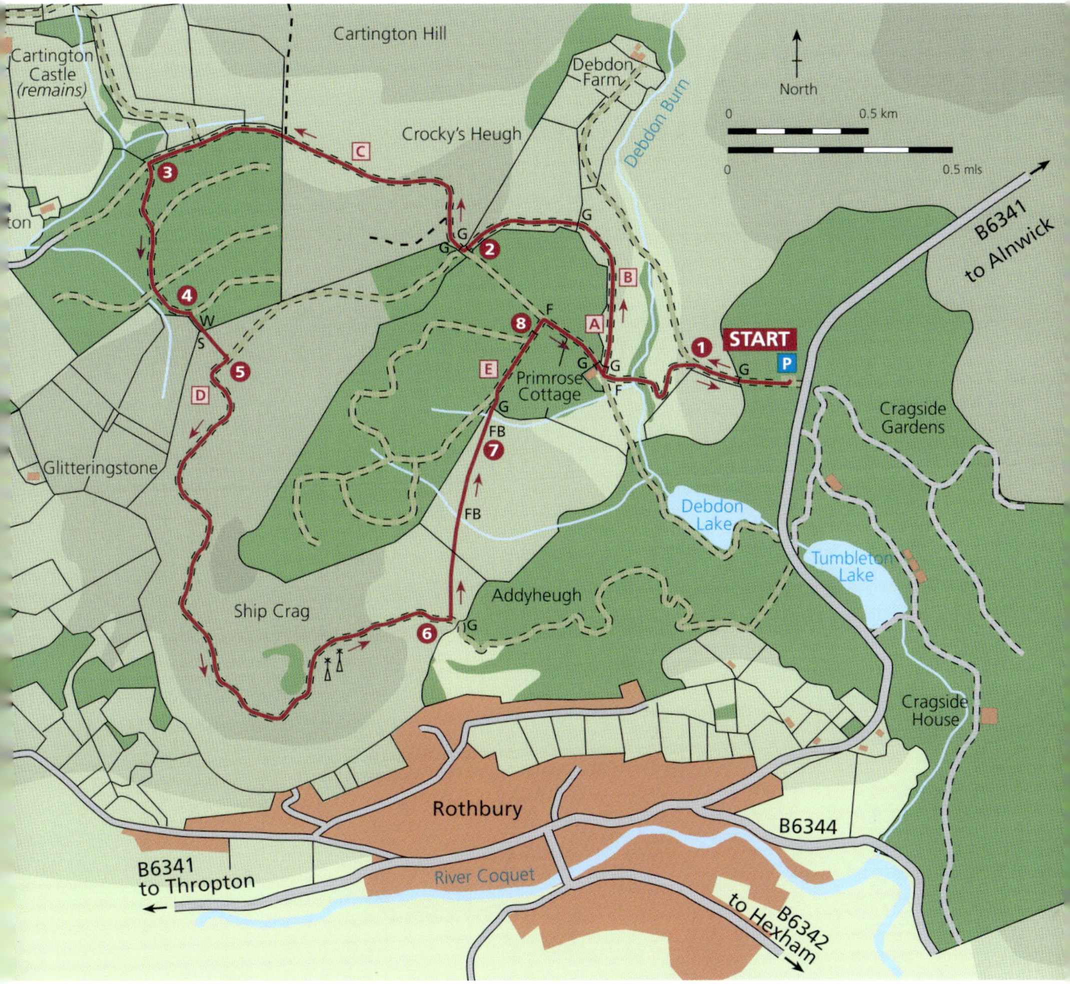

From the parking area, walk along the tarmac track to a gate, then continue along the track across an area of open moorland.

1. At the sign for Debdon Farm, keep left to head downhill and across the bridge over the Debdon Burn. Close to Primrose Cottage, turn right through a gate (signed 'Public Bridleway: Thropton 2¾; Rothbury 4') and walk along the stone track, with a plantation to your left.

2. Go through the first gate, then turn right through another gate and head uphill along a stone track towards Crocky's Heugh. Continue along this track for the next half mile or so.

A In late summer, as the heather comes into flower, the moorlands around Rothbury take on the distinctive purple hue that is so evocative of these wild northern landscapes. At this time of year, beekeepers from across the north of England bring their hives here so that, for a few short weeks, their bees can gather the nectar from the heather flowers and make the prized 'heather honey', with its distinctive taste and texture. The hives are kept in a cool sheltered spot on the moor edge so that the bees are close to the heather and don't have to fly too far, although some may travel several miles if food is in short supply.

Bees have been having a hard time of late. In 1992 *Varroa* mites reached the UK after being first discovered in bee colonies in south east Asia about a century ago. The mites feed off larval, pupal and adult bees and are carriers of a deadly virus that can wipe out hives or colonies of feral bees. Added to the problem of *Varroa*, is the recent emergence of 'Colony Collapse Disorder' when, for no apparent reason, the worker bees desert the hive and just disappear. The cause is unknown, although it is thought that it may be linked to pesticides, diseases or malnutrition. Because so many crops are pollinated by bees, it is having a serious impact on the agricultural industry, especially in the USA.

Bee hives on the edge of the moors close to Primrose Cottage and a worker bee gathering pollen from heather flowers

3 At the Forestry Commission sign for the 'Blue Mill' woodland, turn left and go through the gap beside the forest barrier. Follow the track up the hill through the woodland: much of this is now being felled and replanted. There are a few tracks off to the left and right but just ignore these.

4 As the path levels out and curves to the left, watch out for a 'Public Footpath' waymarker post on the right side of the path. Here, turn right off the track and follow a narrow path beside a stone wall. After about 80 metres, as the wall turns to the left, climb the stone step-stile over the wall and take the path straight ahead. Continue along this path for about 150 metres to reach a wide stone track.

B The well drained acidic soils along the Debdon Burn are ideal for foxgloves *(Digitalis purpurea)* with their distinctive tall stems of purple bell-shaped flowers although, occasionally, these can vary in colour to a pale white. It is a fascinating plant with a sinister reputation: it contains a chemical called digitalin which is highly toxic - the upper leaves are so potent that eating just one or two leaves can cause death - and probably led herbalists to call it Dead Men's Bells or Witches Gloves. Perhaps one of its most famous victims (almost) was James Bond in the 2006 version of Casino Royale when digitalin was slipped into his drink.

In the correct dose, digitalin (in its pure form it is known as digoxin or digitoxin) can be a very powerful drug and is used for the treatment of heart conditions, especially to control cardiac arrhythmia and to slow a patient's heart rate. Its medicinal qualities have been known for centuries but it was little used by herbalists because of the difficulties in calculating the correct dose - although presumably the patients for whom they got the dose wrong didn't often have the opportunity to come back and complain.

C The bright red stone on this track is andesite or 'red whin', a rock that was formed many millions of years ago from the lava produced by a huge volcano centred on what are now the Cheviot Hills. The rock is excavated from the Harden Quarry at Biddlestone which, on a clear day, you may just be able to see, cut into the line of hills in the far distance. It is one of the few places in the UK where this type of stone is actively quarried and, because of its hardness and distinctive colour, it has many different uses, from motorway hard shoulders and cycle paths to domestic gravel drives and military parade grounds. It has even been used to create the longest 'red carpet' in the world - The Mall in London, leading to Buckingham Palace.

On the left side of this track, a few hundred metres before it enters a woodland, there is a lovely old stone parish boundary marker. The letters 'C' and 'R' on either side refer to the parishes of Cartington and Rothbury.

5 At the track, turn right and follow this old 'carriage drive' for the next 1½ miles as it meanders around the western and southern sides of Ship Crag. Past the telecoms and TV masts below Ship Crag, the track curves to the right towards the woodlands at Addyheugh.

6 About 25 metres before a gate into Addyheugh wood, close to a small stone cairn on the left side of the track, turn left along a path that soon drops down to cross a boggy section of moorland.

D The wide stone track that follows the contours around the western and southern sides of Ship Crag is part of an old carriage drive that was built in the late 19th century for Lord Armstrong, the then owner of the Cragside estate. The estate covered over 1700 acres (690 hectares) and, to enable his family and guests to enjoy its beautiful lakes, woodlands and moorlands, he commissioned the construction of some 50 kilometres of stone-surfaced tracks along which they could be driven in the estate's horse-drawn carriages.

Armstrong was a Newcastle-based engineer who had made his name and fortune from the design and manufacture of armaments. He had spent time in Rothbury as a child and had fond memories of the area so, when retirement beckoned, he bought land along the Debdon Burn and spent much of his time developing the Cragside House and Estate. His engineering expertise was put to good use in building a series of lakes capable of generating hydro-electricity which, in turn, powered incandescent light bulbs (a recent invention by Joseph Swan) in the house - with Cragside becoming the first house in the world to have hydro-electric powered lighting. The House and Gardens are now owned by the National Trust and are open most of the year (see **www.nationaltrust.org.uk** for details).

The Simonside Hills from Ship Crag

7. Cross a footbridge over a stream and go through a wicket gate in a fence. A few metres further on, the path joins a wide stone track: here, turn right to follow the track past a copse of old beech trees.

8. At the T-junction, (just past a Forestry Commission barrier) turn right down the stone track signed 'Public Road: Alnwick Rd (B6341)': this leads to a gate close to Primrose Cottage. Go through the gate and walk straight ahead along the track and back to the start.

2. Alnham and the Salter's Road

FROM ALNHAM VILLAGE, a scattered little hamlet on the edge of the Coquet Valley, this walk follows the route of the ancient Salter's Road, northwards into the Cheviot Hills to the remote steading of Ewartly Shank. The views to The Cheviot and Hedgehope are spectacular and make the long - but never steep - climb well worthwhile. The Salter's Road continues on into Scotland, but from here the walk returns to Alnham via minor roads and bridleways, following the attractive little valley of the Spartley Burn.

OS Map: *1:25000 Outdoor Leisure Map OL16 (The Cheviot Hills)*
Start: *NT 991109*
Grade: *Strenuous*
Length: *5.9 miles (9.5 km) and about 4 hours*
Ascent: *270 metres (885 feet), mostly in the first half of the walk*

Local services
- Rothbury & Powburn
- Netherton, Alwinton & Glanton
- Rothbury & Powburn

To get to Alnham from Rothbury (9 miles), drive along the B6341 to Thropton, turn right and follow the signs to Netherton, then turn right at the far end of the village (in front of the First School) and follow the signs to Alnham. From Powburn (7 miles), go via the minor roads through Glanton, Great Ryle and Prendwick. At Alnham, turn up the minor road to Ewartly Shank and Castle Hill. Drive along this road for ¼ mile and park on the grass verge on the right hand side of the road in front of the church.

Walk along the road for a few metres past the vicarage and its pele tower (in Northumberland a pele tower is an old fortified manor house) and turn right (signed 'Public Bridleway: Shank House 3; Low Bleakhope 5') across a small stream and along a track beside the vicarage garden wall.

1 Go through a gate and follow the path uphill, with a drystone wall on your left. Continue straight ahead along this path through two more gates, with plantations to your right and then left.

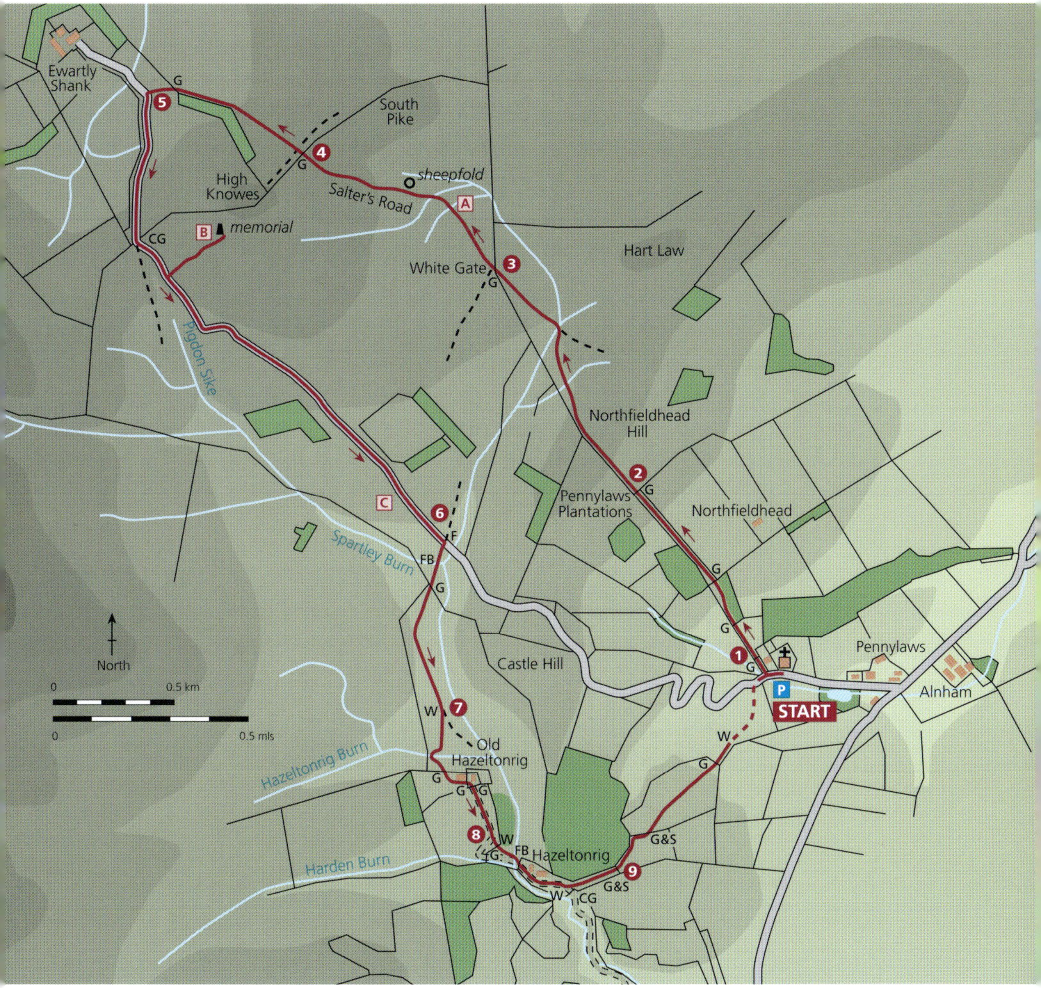

2 At the moorland edge, go through the wicket gate and continue uphill, with the stone wall still close by on your left. Over the brow of Northfieldhead Hill, keep to the path as it veers to the right, away from the wall. Across the second, and larger, of two streams, the path turns slightly left and heads for a gate in a stone wall about 300 metres away: this is 'White Gate'.

3 Through 'White Gate', continue straight ahead along the wide (but sometimes indistinct) route of the 'Salters Road' which, after about 500 metres, takes you just to the left of a large stone sheepfold. From the sheepfold, the path is a lot clearer and heads uphill over the saddle between High Knowes and South Pike.

A This track across the Cheviot Hills was once one of the main transport routes over the border between England and Scotland and is called the Salter's Road. It is thought that it acquired its name during the mediaeval period (1066 – 1540) when it was used by salt traders. The salt was produced at the coast and then taken by packhorse through Rothbury to Alnham, and then across the Cheviots into Scotland. At this time salt was a precious commodity and traders could grow rich on the proceeds.

The Salter's Road is one of several ancient trade routes across these hills with most, such as 'Clennel Street' and 'The Street', having their origins as drove roads for herding cattle from southern Scotland to markets in England. The drovers were local men and, in late spring, would start to visit farms, bargaining for cattle often only one or two at a time, since many of the highland farming tenants were very poor. Gradually, as summer advanced, they would have a herd they could gather and drive south. The herds would be at least 100 strong, or larger, and could number as many as 2000. The journeys were often hazardous but, like the trade in salt, it had the potential to be very rewarding. This trade carried on through into the 19th century but, with the advent of motor transport for livestock haulage, these rural byways were abandoned and are now used only by the occasional posse of walkers.

Along the Salter's Road to Ewartly Shank and the Cheviot Hills

4 Go through the gate in the fence line and follow the path downhill, keeping to the right of the plantation: this takes you through another gate at the bottom of the plantation and down to a tarmac road, close to Ewartly Shank.

5 Turn left along the road and follow this to the top of the hill and across a cattle grid. From a point 200 metres beyond the cattle grid, you can take a short detour uphill to the left to the stone memorial to two local shepherds who died near here in a blizzard in November 1962. Continue down the road, heading back towards Alnham.

B The 'Shepherd's Cairn' memorial was erected in 2007 to commemorate two local shepherds, Jock Scott and Willie Middlemas, who died nearby during a blizzard on 17th November 1962. At the time, they were making their way home from Rothbury Mart and dropped off their colleague, Willie Bulloch, at Castle Hill Farm near Alnham. Through one of the worst blizzards in many years, they tried to make their way home by tractor to Ewartly Shank, although at that time the road from Alnham was only a rough track and there was no telephone line to the farm. It was two days before it was realised that they were missing and a full scale search was mounted involving the police and RAF, together with local shepherds and farm workers. The tractor was found abandoned and Jock's body was discovered a day later buried in a snow drift close to this spot on the slopes of High Knowes. Willie's body was found shortly afterwards about 100 metres away.

One of the positive outcomes of this sad story is that it prompted the formation of the Northumberland National Park Mountain Rescue - a volunteer organisation that turns out in all weathers to help save lives in some of the remotest parts of the Northumberland uplands.

6 At the bottom of the hill, just before the road crosses a bridge over a stream, turn right along a wide path (signed 'Public Bridleway: Old Hazeltonrig ¾; Hazeltonrig 1')*. This leads to a footbridge over the Spartley Burn and, a few metres further on, to a pair of gates in a fence. Go through the left-hand gate and follow the path to the left, which runs along the bluff above the Spartley Burn. (* Instead, if you are short of time, you can just continue straight on along the road, past Castle Hill, and back to your car).

C On these hill grasslands, two of the commonest breeds of sheep are the 'Blackface' and the 'Cheviot'. As their name implies, Blackface sheep have a black face but they are also distinctive in having horns, whilst the Cheviots have a white face, a 'Roman' nose and no horns. When the two breeds are 'crossed', the appearance of the lambs will be somewhere between the two. The Blackface is probably the most numerous breed of sheep in the British uplands and is renowned for its ability to tolerate a harsh climate and thrive on different types of land. The Cheviot breed is also very hardy and originated here in north Northumberland: their high quality wool was once the foundation for the Border Tweed industry. The advantage of crossing these two breeds is that the offspring can inherit favourable traits from both parents.

In recent decades sheep farmers have been hit by the triple whammy of increasing costs, a collapse in the demand for wool and competition from cheap lamb imports. The current trend towards reduced stocking levels and producing high quality lamb for local markets is helping to stabilise prices and could breathe new life into hill sheep farming.

Above: Blackface ewes on the hills above Alnham: these have been mated with a Cheviot tup (ram) to produce cross-bred lambs.

Right: A blackface tup at Old Hazeltonrig

North along the Spartley Burn towards Hogden Law

7 At a waymarker post, bear right along an indistinct grass path that heads towards a gate in a fence line to the right of the farm buildings at Old Hazeltonrig. (The left fork, which heads to the left of Old Hazeltonrig, is a more distinct path but should be ignored). The path drops down to cross a stream, then climbs the far side to the gate in the fence. Go through the gate and bear left to pass close to the buildings and through a pair of gates (the first is often left open) to a stone track through a field.

8 As the stone track turns right, bear left to follow the waymarked route of the public bridleway through a wicket gate and then down to cross a footbridge over the Spartley Burn before re-joining the track. Go past the farm cottages at Hazeltonrig: on the far side of the brick-built cottage, ignore the 'Public Footpath' waymarker pointing off to the left and continue along the track for another 40 metres to a 'Public Bridleway' waymarker: here, turn left off the track and follow a grass path heading steeply uphill close to a line of electricity poles.

9 Go through a gate at the top of the hill and bear left along the edge of a field beside a wood: this brings you to a stile beside a gate. Over the stile, bear half-right across the field, following the line of a faint ridge (as shown by the waymarker disc on the gate post). Through a gate at the bottom of the field, continue down to the road, following the waymarked 'Permissive Footpath'. At the road, turn right over the cattle grid and back to the start.

3. Old Bewick and Blawearie

AN ANCIENT TRACK HEADS EAST FROM THE VILLAGE OF OLD BEWICK and takes you to the ruins of the abandoned farm steading at Blawearie - a sad and atmospheric reminder of the heyday of hill farming in the early 20th century. From here, the walk follows the Harehope Burn, past an Iron Age hillfort, then skirts around the side of Bewick Hill and Hanging Crag to take you back to Old Bewick. The banks of rhododendron that cover the southern side of Bewick Hill are spectacular in early summer so put this walk in your diary for late May or early June.

OS Map: *1:25000 Explorer Map 332 (Alnwick and Amble)*
Start: *NU 066215*
Grade: *Fairly easy*
Length: *4.0 miles (6.5 km) and about 2½ hours*
Ascent: *200 metres (660 feet) on gentle gradients*

Local services
- Powburn
- Eglingham, Powburn & Glanton
- Powburn

The walk starts at Old Bewick, a small village situated about 3 miles to the west of Eglingham, off the B6346. Park on the north side of the road, taking care not to obstruct any of the access tracks to the farm or the cottages.

Walk up the stone track in front of the farm cottages (signed 'Public Bridleway: Blawearie 1½ Quarry House 3½'). At the end of the farm buildings go through a gate and straight on along the track, ignoring the path to the left signed to 'Bewick Folly'.

1 Go through the gate below the old pine trees on Hanging Crag and stay on the track, keeping a drystone wall to your left. A few hundred metres further on the track takes you through another gate.

A A few yards up the track from Old Bewick there stands a lovely old crab apple tree that, over the years, must have helped to keep generations of local villagers well supplied with crab apple jelly and fed many a blackbird and thrush in the early autumn. It used to be thought that all of the different varieties of cultivated apples grown in the UK were descended from the native crab apple. Recent genetic research has traced the origin of all of the world's apples back to a single species, *Malus sieversii*, that grows wild in the forests of the Celestial Mountains on Kazakhstan's border with China. Sadly, many of these forests were destroyed during the years of Soviet rule when much of the land was cleared for intensive farming as part of the campaign to open up 'virgin lands'. The Kazakh government now recognizes the importance of the forests that remain, not least because the name of its former capital city, Almaty, translates as 'Father of Apples', and efforts are being made to conserve them from the new threats of oil exploration and tourism development.

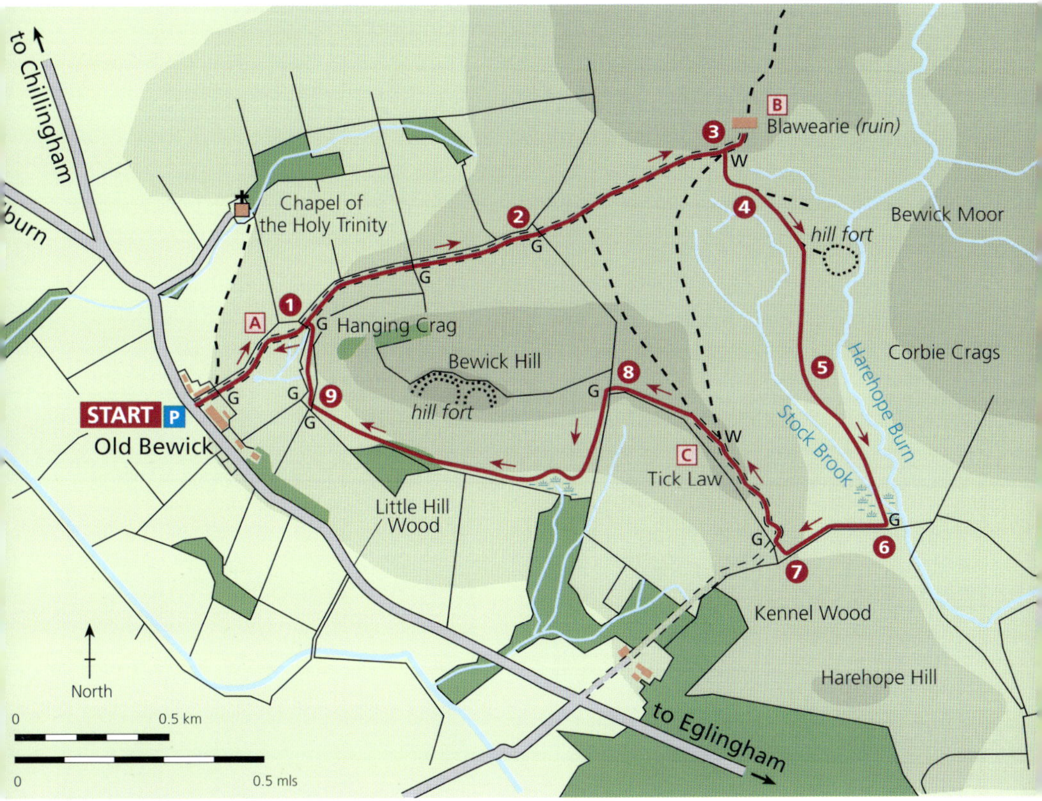

From the track to Blawearie, looking back towards Bewick Hill and the Cheviots

2 Go through a wicket gate beside a field gate and keep straight on along the track towards Blawearie.

3 About 200 metres short of Blawearie, turn right at a waymarker post, following the direction indicated by the yellow arrow on the 'Public Footpath' waymarker disc (i.e. of the two paths heading south from this point, take the one that forks to the left – see map). Before doing so, it is worth taking a few minutes to have a look at the ruins of the old farm steading.

B When the mists are down, the ruined farm buildings at Blawearie can be an atmospheric and slightly spooky place. They are also a sad reminder of a time when the farms and villages of England's northern uplands were bustling with life and supported far larger populations than they do today. The people who built the farm here chose a good spot, being sheltered from the worst of the winter weather, which comes from the north and east, and having its own spring, which still seeps out of the rocks nearby. Blawearie was last occupied in the 1930s, when the daughter of the farmer - who probably took the old photograph below - used to walk to school in Old Bewick. After the farm was abandoned at the beginning of World War II, it was used by the army for training exercises but soon became derelict and the roofs and some of the walls were taken down for safety reasons. Once the weather could get in, its decline accelerated and all that are left today are a derelict shell and a reminder of a way of life that has gone forever.

Blawearie today and as it looked in the 1930s when it was still a working hill farm

Harehope Burn

4 About 230 metres from the waymarker post at Blawearie, the path forks: at this point, keep to the right and head over a low ridge. From the far side of this ridge, you can take a short detour to the left to look at the Iron Age hillfort, strategically located on a promontory above the Harehope Burn: the earth ramparts are still intact and give you a good impression of how its defences were designed. The route of your walk continues on a distinct grass path running steadily downhill, with the Harehope Burn a few hundred metres over to the left – along this section of the walk there are several smaller paths heading off to left and right but ignore these and keep to the main track.

5 Over the brow of a gorse covered knoll, the path continues downhill, keeping close to the top of the ridge between the Harehope Burn and the Stock Brook. At the bottom of the hill, the path picks its way through a boggy patch of ground (take care – this can be wet and quite treacherous) and across the Stock Brook, then heads for a wicket gate in a fence line.

6 Immediately in front of the wicket gate, turn right onto a path along the edge of the heather, with a fence to your left.

7 On reaching the fence line running down from Tick Law, turn sharp right up the hill, keeping the fence to your left. After a few metres, at a gate in the fence, turn right along a sunken track that winds its way uphill. From the summit of Tick Law, keep close to the fence line on your left: this leads to a wicket gate in a stone wall on the east side of Bewick Hill. (Note: on Tick Law be sure NOT to take either of the two paths to the right - the first of which is waymarked - heading back across the moor towards Blawearie.)

8 Through the wicket gate, turn left. Towards the bottom of the hill, the path curves to the right, then loops above a patch of rushes and back down to run close to a stone wall. Past Little Hill Wood, the path continues around the side of the hill.

9 Go through the first of two field gates, then bear right up the hill, around a fence corner and over the remains of a tumbled-down stone wall. Continue along the path around the side of the hill, keeping a fence, then a wall, to your left. This leads back to the track followed on the outward leg of your walk. Turn left through the gate below Hanging Crag and back to Old Bewick.

C The rhododendrons that cover the southern slopes of Bewick Hill look beautiful in late spring and provide a colourful contrast to the different shades of green cast by dense beds of bracken and scattered birch and rowan trees. Rhododendron, *Rhododendron ponticum*, is not native to the British Isles but was introduced from eastern Asia by Victorian gardeners, always eager to find new and exotic plants with which to impress their friends. In some parts of the country they 'escaped' from these domestic confines to become established on moors and heaths where the acidic peaty soils were very much to their liking. Unfortunately rhododendrons have little value beyond their colourful appearance since they are completely inedible to livestock, suppress most other ground vegetation and are of little value to wildlife. In some parts of the country such as Snowdonia, rhododendron has colonised extensive tracts of countryside, defying most attempts to eradicate it.

Rhododendrons on the slopes of Bewick Hill, viewed from Tick Law

4. Chillingham Park and Ros Castle

CHILLINGHAM PARK IS FAMOUS FOR ITS WILD CATTLE but this walk offers you the chance to explore and enjoy much more of this beautiful estate. The first half is a fairly strenuous climb and takes you close to the summit of Ros Castle: here there is a picnic seat with what must be one of the most spectacular views in Northumberland, so save your sandwiches till then. From there, it's all downhill, winding through woodlands and parklands back to the start. Please note that this walk is all on private land and NO DOGS are allowed.

Along the walk you may catch a glimpse of the Chillingham wild cattle. If you want to see them at close quarters, go on one of the guided tours with the Warden advertised on the notice boards close to the car park (Note: Route directions 1 and 2 for this walk take you to the tour start.)

OS Map: *1:25000 Explorer Map 340 (Holy Island and Bamburgh)*
Start: *NU 062260*
Grade: *Strenuous*
Length: *5.0 miles (8.0 km) and about 3 hours*
Ascent: *245 metres (800 feet): all on the first half of the walk, with some fairly steep sections*

Local services
Wooler
Chatton, Wooler
Wooler

Chillingham is a small village situated on a minor road 1½ miles to the south of Chatton. It is easy to find because the Chillingham 'Wild Cattle' are well signed off the A697 and the A1. To get to the start of the walk, turn up the side road in the centre of the village, indicated by the 'Wild Cattle' signs (not the entrance gate signed to 'Chillingham Castle' about ¼ mile further south). Just after the road bends to the left at a side entrance to the castle, park on the left hand side beneath the signs 'Parking for Wild Cattle'.

At the far end of the parking area, close to a small cottage, turn right up a track signed 'Forest Walk' (look for a finger post on top of an old tree stump). This leads to a gateway in a high stone wall and then bears left up a wide stone track: after about 200 metres, carry straight on up the hill through another gateway (ignoring both the track that turns sharp right and the gate on the left). On the right hand side of this gateway you will see a carved bone arrow on a 'Forest Walk' finger post - the Chillingham Park Estate uses these as waymarkers, so keep an eye out for them along the route of this walk.

1 At the edge of a wood, go through a wicket gate and head diagonally to the right, across a field in the direction indicated by an arrow on top of the gate post. Following the 'Wild Cattle' signs, head for a gate at the bottom corner of the field.

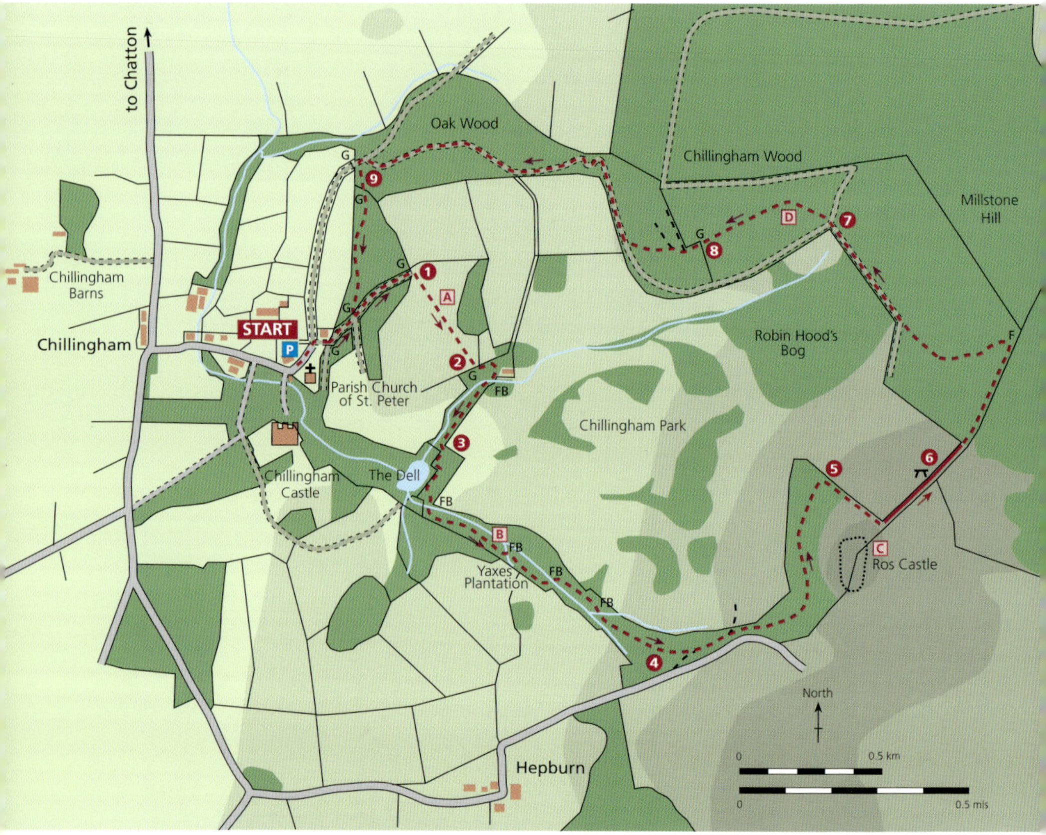

Parish Church of St Peter at Chillingham

2 Through the gate, turn left along a path through the trees towards an old stone barn. (If you want to take one of the tours with the Warden to see the Chillingham Wild Cattle at close quarters, these start from the small shed beside the barn.) About 20 metres before the barn (and ignoring the signs for 'Forest Walk' and 'Wild Cattle' heading left) follow the path to the right which, after about 50 metres, crosses a timber footbridge over a stream. Follow the path along the edge of a wood with a high fence on your left.

A Chillingham bull

A The Chillingham wild cattle are quite unique in that they have lived within the confines of Chillingham Park for over 700 years. The origins of the herd are unknown but one theory is that they are descended from aurochs, an extinct type of wild cattle that once roamed across Europe, Asia and North Africa. It is thought that some of these cattle were enclosed within the Park in the 13th century to provide food and hide for local people. They have been here ever since and, with no other types of cattle ever having been bred into the herd, they are still genetically pure. In common with many wild animals, life within the herd boils down to 'survival of the fittest' and they all live and die within the Park. Severe winters can temporarily reduce numbers, but the herd is now fit and healthy and about 70 strong - a number that the food and shelter within the Park is able to sustain.

3 Towards the bottom of the wood, the path doglegs around a couple of fence corners, then turns sharp left, and sharp right, close to a lake. About 100 metres further on, and with an old metal gate visible 40 metres ahead, take the path left (signed 'Forest Walk') through a plantation. Across a timber footbridge over a stream, follow the path left through a wood, with the stream to your left and a high fence to your right. This path winds its way uphill through the wood, with occasional carved bone waymarkers confirming the route.

B As some fields come into view on the right, the path passes between two very tall trees: these form part of a row of four trees which, from right to left, are Wellingtonia, Silver Fir, Douglas Fir, Hemlock. This part of the estate was once planted as an arboretum and still retains many fascinating species of trees, especially conifers, from all parts of the world. The single tree to the right of the path is a Wellingtonia (*Sequoiadendron giganteum*). Better known as the 'Giant Sequoia or 'California Redwood', this species originates in the Sierra Nevada mountains in the western United States where it can reach over 100 metres in height and 27 metres in girth and can live for up to 3,400 years. They don't grow anything like that tall in the British climate, with the largest specimens being only about 50 metres high. In Scotland and northern England the Wellingtonia is sometimes called the 'thumpy tree' because the bark is so soft that you can 'thump' it with your fist with (relative) impunity – just make sure you've got the right tree before you have a go and don't hit it too hard!

4 As a road-side stone wall comes into view on the right, keep to the main path continuing uphill through the wood. Eventually the path curves to the left and gradually levels off to follow the contour around the west side of Ros Castle.

5 At the end of the wood, turn sharp right in front of a gate and climb uphill along the woodland edge. At a stone wall at the top of the hill, turn left along a moorland path between the wall and a fence: a small seat about 250 metres along this path is a great place for a rest and a picnic lunch, with fabulous views over north Northumberland. It is possible to take a detour up to the top of Ros Castle but the view is just as good from the little seat and, looking back, it actually gives you a better perspective of the Iron Age hillfort on the summit.

C Ros Castle is an Iron Age hillfort dating from the first millennium BC. Such hillforts are quite common across upland Northumberland and feature in a number of the walks in this book (see also Walk No. 5 to 'The Ringses' on Doddington Moor and Walk No. 6 to 'Yeavering Bell' near Kirknewton). These forts were primarily defensive in nature, providing a place of refuge for local people, although they may also have served as a status symbol to 'impress the neighbours' and demonstrate the power and influence of a local clan.

Ros Castle is a stunning example, occupying a commanding position on top of the highest hill in the area and giving its former inhabitants an all-round field of view. Its defences comprised a single stone and earth rampart, with a ditch around the south and east sides: inside the fort, the outlines of at least two round-houses have been found. Looking back to Ros Castle from the picnic seat affords a very good view of the profile of the ramparts and helps one appreciate how much manual work must have gone into their construction.

6 From the seat, continue along the moorland path: this soon enters a forest, taking you downhill alongside a high stone wall. In late July and early August the bilberries growing on the right hand side of the path offer a tempting, if messy, finish to your picnic. At a gap in the wall, turn sharp left down the path through the trees, signed to 'Chillingham'. The path winds its way downhill through the wood following waymarker posts. Close to Robin Hood's Bog, the path joins a wider track coming from the left: here, bear right, heading towards Chillingham Wood.

7 Go straight across a wide stone track and through a wicket gate in a high fence (signed to 'Chillingham'). This takes you along a lovely shady path through a young plantation.

Above: A Painted Lady butterfly sunning itself on the path through Chillingham Wood

Left: From the path up to Ros Castle, looking over Chillingham Wood, with the Northumberland coast in the far distance

D The path through Chillingham Wood is one of the most peaceful and attractive sections of the walk. This woodland was planted in the 1990's and is a good example of how commercial forestry can be balanced with the creation of woodlands that are both visually appealing and valuable for wildlife. The main species are oak and Scots pine with a few Sitka spruce and some self-sown birch and rowan. The long term aim will be to create an oak woodland, but the pines have been planted as a 'nurse' crop to shelter and protect the young oaks in the early years and, by planting them close together, the oaks will be encouraged to grow up towards the light, deterring the growth of side branches which would reduce the quality of the timber. Over the years the pine and spruce will be gradually removed to provide some income for the estate and prevent the oaks becoming too crowded. Eventually, even the oak trees will be thinned out to select only those trees that have the straightest and cleanest stems (i.e. least side branches - and hence fewest knots in the timber): these will then be grown on to produce the final crop, which will probably be felled in about 100 years time.

8 Go through a wicket gate in another high fence. About 100 metres further on, as the path curves to the right and heads downhill, the path forks: here, bear left, to follow a steep path leading down to a wide stone track. Turn right and walk along the track for the next ¾ mile.

9 At a gateway (signed 'Private: No Through Road'), turn left across a small timber footbridge and onto a narrow path winding through a wood: the route is indicated by waymarker posts. At the end of the wood, go through a gate and turn right, down the track to return to the car park.

Bluebells in Yaxes Plantation

5. Doddington Moor

DODDINGTON MOOR IS AN ISOLATED PLATEAU OF MOORLAND on the eastern edge of the Milfield Plain. Long ago this land was occupied by ancient Britons who recognised its strategic position overlooking the fertile lands below and evidence of their passing can still be seen in the remains of hillforts, rock carvings and stone circles. This short walk lets you sample some of this history whilst also offering splendid views across to the Cheviot Hills and letting you enjoy the peace, solitude and fresh air of the Northumberland uplands.

OS Map: *1:25000 Explorer Map 340 (Holy Island and Bamburgh)*
Start: *NT 998326*
Grade: *Fairly easy, although there is a stiff climb at the start*
Length: *3.9 miles (6.2 km) and about 2½ hours*
Ascent: *150 metres (500 feet): all on the first section up to Shepherd's House*

Local services Fenton Centre, Wooler, Milfield
Wooler & Milfield
Wooler & Milfield

The walk starts at Doddington Village, which lies about 3 miles north of Wooler on the B6525. At the village, turn down the side road signed to Nesbit and Fentons. After about 100 metres, follow the road round to the right and park on the wide grass verge on the right side of the road. Across the road there is a small kiosk selling Doddington Dairy's home-made (and now famous) ice cream and cheese. Both are delicious, and the promise of an ice cream at the end of the walk should serve as a useful bribe for any foot-dragging by recalcitrant children (or adults).

Walk back up to the main road, cross over to the far side (taking care to watch out for oncoming traffic), turn right and walk along the roadside verge. As the road curves to the right near the edge of the village, take the road left signed to Wooler Golf Club.

Doddington Village

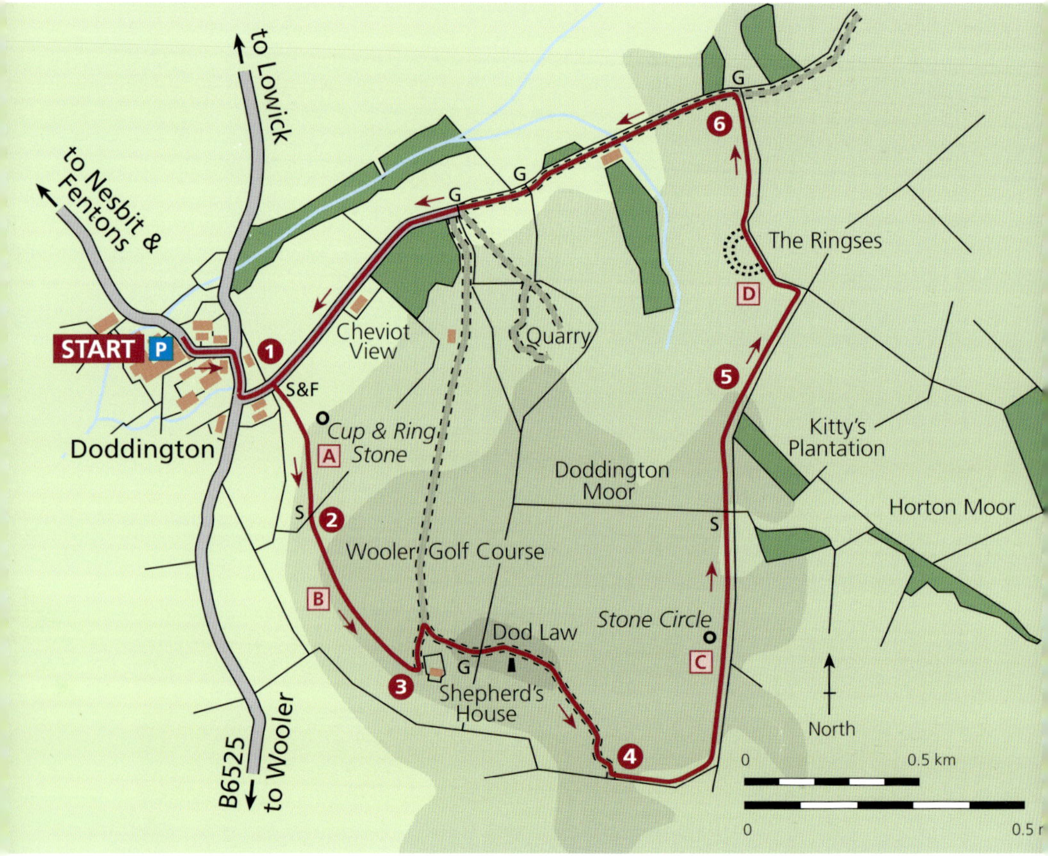

1 Just past the cottages on the right, turn right over a stile (signed 'Public Footpath: West Horton 2¼; Dod Law ½; Weetwood Hill 2'). From the stile, head straight uphill between two hawthorn bushes. Over the first brow, bear slightly right towards a group of old hawthorns about 200 metres further up the hill – during the summer the path can become hidden in the bracken but the hawthorns that you are aiming for are always in view. On reaching the hawthorns, you will see that they are growing on a low ridge that heads in a straight line diagonally uphill to the right: follow this ridge to a stile in a fence.

A 'Cup and Ring' marked rock is a few metres away from the line of hawthorns. To see it, turn back sharp left from the first hawthorn bush of the line, and follow the contour, heading towards the little cottage (Cheviot View) in the distance. The cup and ring marked rock is about 90 metres away.

A 'Cup and Ring' marked stones date from the Bronze Age (2100BC - 700BC), or possibly earlier, and are scattered across the uplands of northern England and southern Scotland. This is a fairly modest example but you can still pick out the concentric rings that are typical of this type of prehistoric 'rock art'. For more information, please see page 52 of this book which describes the far more impressive rock carvings at Routin Linn, which are visited on Walk 8.

2 Climb over the stile in the fence and follow the well defined path that continues uphill. This gradually levels out and runs around the side of the hill to Shepherd's House.

From the path to Shepherd's House, looking north over Doddington Village

B The flat expanse of the Milfield Plain extends out to the west, with the River Till meandering through the lush and fertile arable fields that in the summer months grow swathes of wheat, barley and rape. About 25,000 years ago, towards the end of the last Ice Age, the plain was a huge lake fed by meltwaters from the glaciers that covered the Cheviot Hills. The clay and silt deposited in the lake bed formed the rich soils that are now the lifeblood of farming in the area.

During the Second World War, the flat land of the Milfield Plain was seen as an ideal site for the establishment of an RAF airfield where fighter planes, such as Hurricanes and Typhoons, could be stationed to intercept Luftwaffe bombers attacking from Norway. Later in the war it became one of the main centres for the Fighter Leaders School and Air Support Course where aircrew were trained in the air-to-air air-to-ground attack methods vital for control of the Normandy beach-heads and the subsequent advance through Europe. The airfield was manned by pilots of many nationalities and the tombstones of some of the airmen killed in action or training can still be seen in Kirknewton churchyard on the northern edge of the Cheviot Hills.

3 At Shepherd's House, turn left along a wide grass track. After about 130 metres this brings you to the edge of the golf course*: here, turn right and then, after 10 metres, turn right again along another wide grass track that heads across the moor towards Dod Law. Climb over a stile beside a gate to continue along the track and past the concrete trig point that marks the summit of Dod Law. Follow the track down to a gate in a fence at the edge of the moor. [*Note: if you want to see another cup and ring marked rock, turn left here and walk about 80 metres along the edge of the golf course: the rock is just in the rough grass on your left. Take care to watch for golfers driving from the tees to your right]

4 Immediately in front of the gate, turn left and walk along a path beside a fence. At the field corner, where the fence meets a stone wall, turn left along the wall. The path takes you past an old stone circle and then over a stile in a fence.

C Stonehenge it certainly isn't - but the small stone circle on the east side of Doddington Moor may be just as old, probably dating from the Neolithic Period (about 3000BC - 2000BC). Nobody knows why these stone circles were built but theories abound, with the most popular being that they were shrines to worship ancestors or were a form of calendar to mark summer and winter solstices. It has also been suggested that they may have marked the site of mediaeval social gatherings where communities came together to exchange goods, to settle disputes or perhaps to seek marriage partners. In the past they have often been associated with the Druids but it is now known that they were built some 2500 years before the earliest known reference to the Druids.

The Doddington stone circle originally had five stones, of which three remain, with only one still standing upright: the deeply weathered rainwater channels on the top of this stone give some clue as to how long it must have been here.

East towards Horton Moor

5 Past Kitty's Plantation the ramparts of The Ringses Iron Age Hillfort come into view over to the left. At the next fence line, turn left and follow the fence. This curves around to the right past The Ringses then takes you downhill to meet a stone track. It worth taking a detour from the route of the walk to explore The Ringses.

D North Northumberland is one of the best places in the UK to see the remains of Iron Age hillforts - defended settlements built by ancient Britons about 2000 years ago. Most Iron Age Britons were farmers and made a living from growing crops and raising livestock but these were unsettled times, and feuding between neighbouring tribes would have been common. Across the uplands of Northumberland, hillforts were constructed to provide protection and security for people and their livestock. Most were strategically located on hilltops and ridges to provide a good field of view over the surrounding land and conformed to a fairly standard design, with one or more outer ramparts enclosing a central area in which were constructed the 'round houses' of the inhabitants. These hillforts were probably occupied for several centuries, and in some cases through the Roman occupation, only being finally abandoned in the Middle Ages.

The Ringses Iron Age hillfort is defended by a steep slope to the west, with three semi-circular earth and stone ramparts. The original entrance lies through the south-east side (the direction from which you will approach the fort) but there are also three other gaps in the ramparts which were added some time later. Inside the hillfort, archaeologists have found the foundations of at least three round-houses.

6 At the track, turn left. Follow the track through a gate and on past the entrance to Wooler Golf Club. This takes you down to the main road in Doddington Village and back to the car.

6. Yeavering Bell and the Akeld Valley

THE IRON AGE HILLFORT ON THE SUMMIT OF YEAVERING BELL is probably the largest and most impressive in the north of England and, although the climb is hard and steep, it is well worth it. The walk then takes you over White Law before dropping down into the remote and beautiful Akeld Valley. The climb up to the head of the valley follows a good stone track and from here its mostly downhill with views northwards across the River Glen and on into Scotland.

OS Map: *1:25000 Outdoor Leisure Map OL16 (The Cheviot Hills)*
Start: NT 924303
Grade: *Very strenuous – with some long and steep climbs*
Length: *6.2 miles (10.0 km) and about 4 hours*
Ascent: *430 metres (1400 feet): the climb up Yeavering Bell is steep and not for the faint-hearted*

Local services
- Akeld, Wooler, Milfield, Heatherslaw Mill & Etal
- Wooler, Milfield & Etal
- Wooler & Milfield

From Wooler, take the A697 north towards Coldstream. At the village of Akeld, about 2½ miles from Wooler, turn left along the B6351 signed to Yeavering, Kirknewton and Yetholm. After a further 2¼ miles, as the road bends sharply to the right, turn left onto a stone track towards the farm cottages at Old Yeavering and park on the wide grass verge on the left hand side.

Walk up the track past the cottages, go through a gate and continue along the track (signed 'Public Footpath: Hethpool 2½; Commonburn Ho 2¾') past an old stone barn.

From the slopes of Yeavering Bell, south west towards Torleehouse and Hethpool

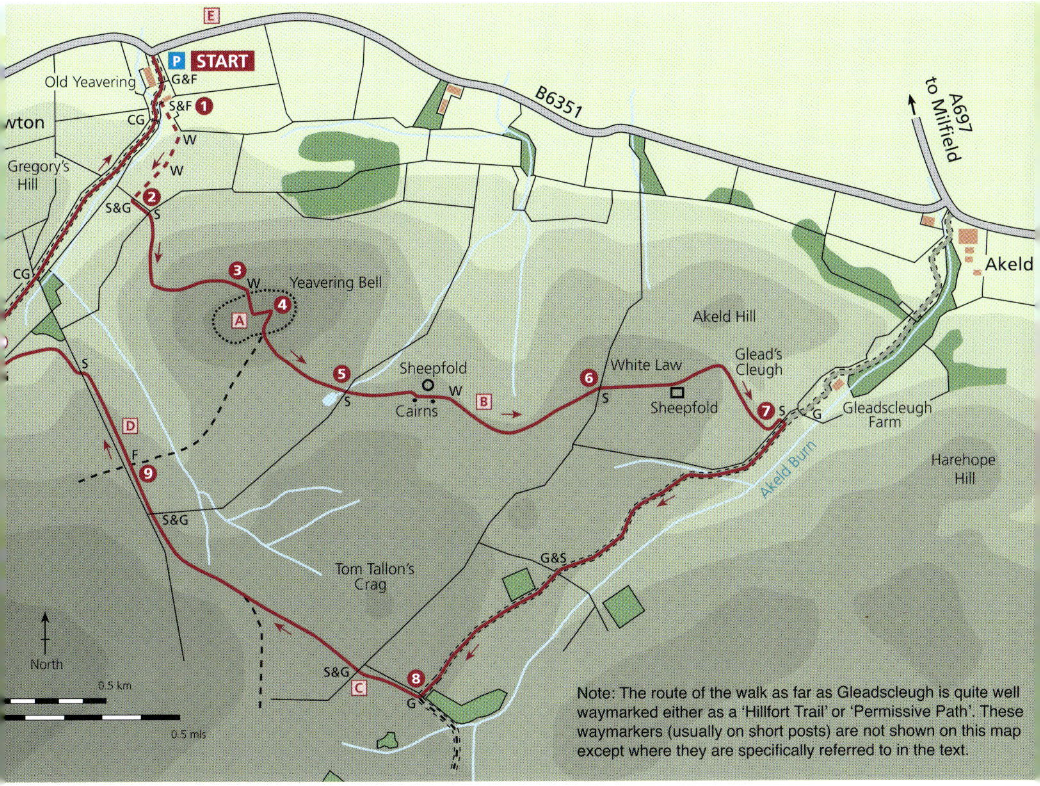

1 On the far side of the old barn, turn left over a stile beside a gate (signed 'Permissive Path: Yeavering Bell ¾') and walk up a grass track. As the track turns left at the field corner, take the path uphill to the right, waymarked 'Hillfort Trail'. At the brow of the next ridge, another waymarker points you straight ahead towards a gate and a ladder stile in an old stone wall.

2 Over the stile, turn sharp left uphill. After about 100 metres, climb over a stile in a fence and follow the waymarked path that bears slightly right, uphill. The path up Yeavering Bell is well defined and there are frequent waymarkers. At the start, it runs diagonally to the right, up the side of the hill, but then it turns left and heads more directly for the summit. About two thirds of the way up, the path crosses an ancient tumbled-down stone wall running up the face of the hill.

3 Close to the summit the path turns to the right (at a waymarker post) to take you through a gap in the stone ramparts of the hillfort. It then heads over a saddle between the twin summits. At the mid-point of the saddle, turn left and climb up to the cairn on the main summit of Yeavering Bell.

A Northumberland is one of the best places in Britain to see Iron Age hillforts - and few are as impressive as the one on the summit of Yeavering Bell. These forts date from the first millennium BC and were primarily defensive structures, where people could find refuge during periods of conflict, although they may also have served as a status symbol to demonstrate the power and influence of a local clan.

Like many such hillforts, this one had a protective stone rampart (originally about 2.5 metres high) enclosing an area of about 5.6 hectares (about 14 acres), in which there are believed to have been about 130 timber round-houses. Archaeological excavations have shown that these houses varied markedly in size, possibly indicating that some were communal or were perhaps used for storage or for housing livestock. The main entrance to the hillfort lies on the south side and is still visible as a gap in the ramparts - you will walk through this when you leave the hillfort. The south facing slopes below the entrance still show the signs of old cultivation terraces where the fort's inhabitants grew crops such as wheat, barley, hemp and flax or grazed their cattle and sheep. The remains of these terraces are now very difficult to see, except when the sun is very low in the sky and casts long shadows off the faint humps and hollows that still survive.

4 From the summit cairn, cut back to the right, down a path that leads to a gap in the southern ramparts of the hillfort. At this point the path splits: take the left fork heading towards a small pond in the valley below. Half way down, the path goes across a wide grass track, then past the pond (on your right) to a ladder stile in a fence.

5 Over the stile, follow the grass path straight ahead across the moor - the alignment of the route is indicated by an arrow fixed to the stile. The path is indicated by occasional waymarker posts and heads for a stone sheepfold (a small enclosure) in the distance. About 50 metres short of the sheepfold, bear right along an indistinct path to a small stone cairn about 20 metres away. At the cairn, take the path to the left past another cairn and a waymarker post. From here, your next destination, the summit of White Law, lies straight ahead. The path is indistinct at times but it runs around the head of the valley and then goes uphill to the summit, where a ladder stile over a stone wall can be seen silhouetted against the skyline.

Peacock butterfly feeding on heather

Yeavering Bell from the south. The stone ramparts of the Iron Age hillfort can be seen encircling the twin summits. The ridge of flatter ground on the south facing slope below the hillfort still bears the faint marks of old enclosures and field systems where the inhabitants kept livestock and grew crops.

B The bushes that are scattered around the head of the valley are all holly and are an unusual sight out on this open moorland, far way from their usual home in lowland woodlands and hedgerows. Further down the valley there are the remains of old homesteads and enclosures and it is possible that these hollies were planted many years ago to provide winter fodder for the livestock of the farmers who lived here.

Holly has long had an association with Christmas traditions and, with its shiny green leaves and bright red berries, it is still a very popular decoration which can brighten up a house on the dullest winter day. Holly also has a few lesser-known connections with Christmas folklore, such as its power to protect a home from malevolent fairies and, more interestingly (and to be noted for future reference), it was said that whichever of prickly-leaved or smooth-leaved holly was first brought into the house dictated whether the husband or wife respectively would rule the household for the coming year.

6 Go over the stile and keep to the path straight ahead that skirts to the left of a square stone sheepfold. From here, continue straight on over the brow of the ridge ahead. The path soon brings you to the head of a small but very steep and deep valley (Gleads Cleugh): here, turn right and follow the ridge line (with the valley on your left) down to a fence.

7 At the fence, go over a stile and turn right along a stone track heading up the Akeld Valley: follow this for the next 1¼ miles to the head of the valley.

Akeld Valley

8 Go through the gate at the corner of the wood. The stone track continues to the left, but our walk goes right, up a hill alongside a fence: this is the route of St Cuthbert's Way. Past the brow of the hill, climb over a stile in a wall: from here, the path is very clearly defined and continues in a north easterly direction, with Yeavering Bell coming back into view ahead on your right.

C The dry stone wall to the right of the path is built with a local stone called andesite. The wall has been restored in recent years, creating an attractive patchwork of old weathered rocks, now encrusted with white and yellow lichens, set amongst the fresher pinks and mauves of the stones that have been split open or 'worked' during the rebuilding process.

The Cheviot Hills were formed many millions of years ago during a period of intense volcanic activity. Cheviot and Hedgehope, the two highest mountains, which can be seen on the horizon over to the south, are all that remain of an immense volcano, with the surrounding, lower lying hills being created by the lava that flowed out - and formed the rock that we now call andesite. During the Ice Ages that followed, the glaciers gradually ground away at this volcanic landscape to create the gently rolling hills that we see today. The Cheviot Hills have a fascinating and very varied geology and a rummage amongst the boulder and shingle banks that are scattered along the larger streams will turn up many different types and colours of rock.

D St Cuthbert's Way is a 62 mile walk from Melrose in the Scottish Borders to Holy Island on the Northumberland Coast. The route was created with the aim of linking sites that are believed to be connected with the life of one of Britain's most celebrated saints. Cuthbert was born in 635AD in the Scottish Borders and spent his early years as a shepherd on the fells of Lauderdale. At the age of 17 he joined the monastery at Melrose and quickly rose through the ranks to become its third Prior. From Melrose he followed the monastery's founder, St Aidan, to Lindisfarne where, shortly after becoming Prior, he died at the age of 52.

Walkers on St Cuthbert's Way

St Cuthbert's Way passes through some of the most dramatic landscapes of the English and Scottish Borders and usually takes about 4 to 5 days to complete. There are several B&Bs at towns and villages along the way and, for those who want to do it in style, you can arrange for your luggage to be taken between overnight stops. Provided the weather holds, you can be almost guaranteed to find this one of the best long distance walks in northern England.

9 At the footpath 'crossroads', keep straight on alongside the stone wall (signed 'Public Footpath: Old Yeavering 2'). About 500 metres further on, go left over a ladder stile beside a gate, then turn right and follow the grass path as it drops down towards a small wood and then curves to the left to a gate at the end of a stone wall. Go through the gate and down to a wide stone track.

10 Turn right along the track and follow this back to Old Yeavering.

E On completing your walk, it is worth driving the short distance back along the road to Wooler to visit the Ad Gefrin monument and the site of the Anglo-Saxon palace in the field behind, which can be accessed via a nearby gate. In the early 7th century AD, Ad Gefrin was the royal township of King Edwin and his queen Aethelburgh, who ruled a kingdom stretching from the River Humber in the south to the Firth of Forth in the north - from which the ancient kingdom of Northumbria gets its name (i.e. the land to the north of the Humber). In 633/34 the kingdom was attacked and Ad Gefrin destroyed by the Welsh King Cadwallon and Penda, the King of Mercia (an Anglo-Saxon kingdom covering much of the present day Midlands). It was rebuilt by Edwin's successor, King Oswald, only to be burnt down again a few years later. Although the settlement at Ad Gefrin survived these attacks, it never regained its former status and, by the end of the 7th century, had been abandoned. Gradually, all signs of the former palace disappeared and it was only re-discovered in 1949 by an archaeologist studying some aerial photographs of the area. The excavations that followed have revealed a wealth of information about the lives of ancient Britons and allowed the site's early history to be pieced together.

7. St Cuthbert's Cave and Swinhoe

THIS WALK FOLLOWS IN THE FOOTSTEPS OF ST CUTHBERT, one of northern England's most celebrated saints. Starting at the hamlet of Holburn Grange, the walk takes you past St Cuthbert's Cave then continues through woodlands and open fields and pastures to Swinhoe Farm. Past Virgin Hill Wood, with its drifts of spring bluebells, you come to Fawcett Hill where there are impressive distant views of Holy Island (St Cuthbert's former home) and the Northumberland coast. The final stretch follows part of the 'St Cuthbert's Way'.

OS Map: *1:25000 Explorer Map 340 (Holy Island and Bamburgh)*
Start: *NU 051351*
Grade: *Fairly easy, with good hard surfaces for most of the way*
Length: *5.3 miles (8.5 km) and about 3 hours*
Ascent: *140 metres (460 feet)*

Local services Belford
Lowick & Belford
Lowick & Belford

Park in the small grass car park at Holburn Grange. To get there, turn off the Chatton - Holburn road (at a point about 4½ miles north of Chatton) onto the side-road signed to 'St Cuthbert's Cave'. After ½ mile, turn left at the T-junction by Holburn Grange (signed to 'St Cuthbert's Cave and Car Park'): the car park is about 100 metres on the left, at the end of the row of cottages.

Walk out of the car park and turn sharp left up a wide grass track between a pair of hedges.

The old drove road heading north east from Holburn Grange

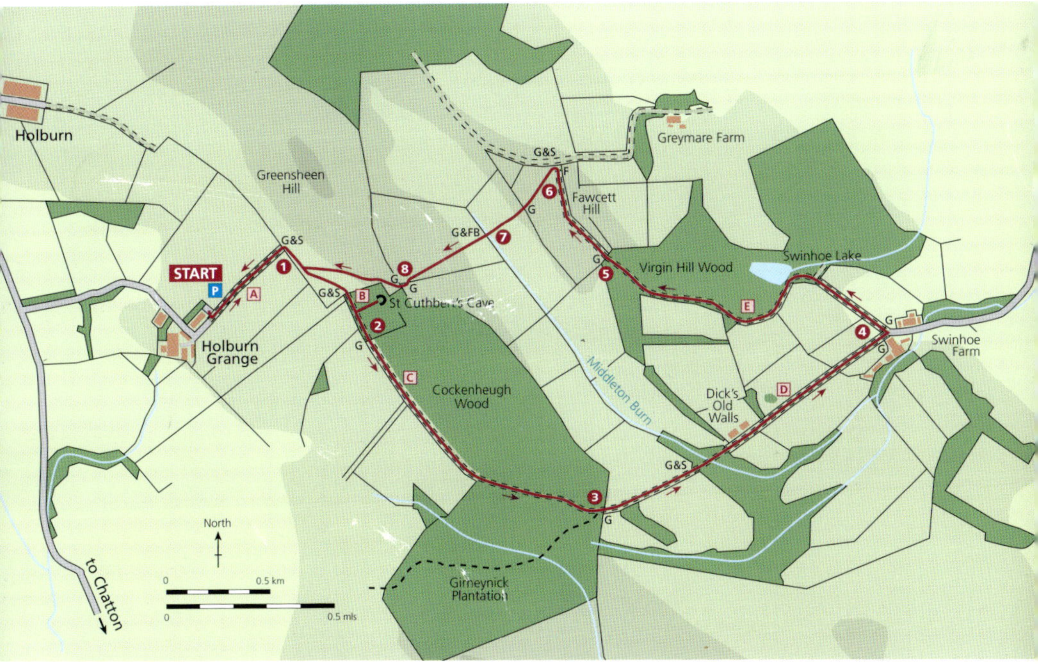

A For such a modest little path, the lane up to the moor (see photograph left) is disproportionately wide, probably signifying that it was once an old drove road. These ancient tracks used to be common across much of northern England and, before the advent of trucks and lorries, were vital for farmers to move their livestock between different seasonal grazings or to drive them to market. Across enclosed farmland the drove roads were essential to prevent livestock straying onto crops but once out on the moor there were no such worries: this is why the lane stops so abruptly at the moorland edge. This drove road would have been part of a network of tracks linking the lowland farms to the west with summer grazings on the higher ground of the Kyloe Hills and may also have connected with other routes over to market towns such as Belford.

In Northumberland some of the principal drove roads were those that crossed the Cheviot Hills, such as 'The Street', 'Clennel Street' and the 'Salter's Road', linking Coquetdale in England with the towns and villages along the Rivers Tweed and Teviot in the Scottish Borders. Walk No. 2 in this book takes you along the 'Salter's Road'.

1 At the top of the track, climb over a stile and turn right. After about 200 metres the path splits – take the right-hand fork and head for a gate at the bottom of a pine wood. Go over a stile beside the gate and about 120 metres further on, turn left up a wide path to St Cuthbert's Cave. After exploring the cave, retrace your steps back to the track along the edge of the pine wood and turn left.

B St Cuthbert's Cave is one of several sites in the English and Scottish Borders that has an historical connection with one of our most celebrated Anglo-Saxon saints - although, in this case, the link is probably rather tenuous. Cuthbert was born in 635AD in the border town of Melrose and, after spending his early years as a shepherd and soldier, he entered holy orders at Melrose Abbey. He quickly rose through the ranks to become Prior of Lindisfarne, where his tact and patience won over many converts to Roman Christianity. In 676, Cuthbert was granted permission by the abbot to retire to a simple life of peace and contemplation as a hermit. Where he spent this time is not known: some suggest the island of Inner Farne (part of the Farne islands, just off the coast near Seahouses) whilst others believe that he chose this cave. However, after nine years, he was persuaded by King Egfrid to return to the monastery on Lindisfarne as its bishop but, by then, the rigours of life as a hermit had taken their toll and he died just two years later at the age of 52. St Cuthbert's bones became one of the monks' most sacred relics and, over the centuries, were carted around much of northern England in an attempt to protect them from Danes, Normans and protestant reformers. Their final resting place was Durham Cathedral, where St Cuthbert's tomb can still be seen.

2 At the end of the pine wood, go through a gate and continue along a wide grass track, with a plantation (Cockenheugh Wood) to your left and fields to your right.

C In early May the ride along the southern edge of Cockenheugh Wood is carpeted in bluebells *(Endymion non-scriptus)*. The bluebell is most commonly found in broadleaved woodland and is one of a small group of plants known as 'woodland indicators', which tend to be found only on land that has been covered in woodland for much of the last 5000 years. The presence of bluebells in this wood tells us that the conifer trees we can see today were planted on a site that, probably until the last century, would have been a fairly natural broadleaved woodland, full of native species such as oak, ash, elm, hawthorn and hazel. Many such woodlands were felled during the two World Wars of the last century when there was a huge demand for timber: then, when they were replanted, conifer species were used because they are much faster growing and therefore produce a quicker economic return.

3 Go through a wicket gate (beside a field gate) and, with the sea in the distance, keep following the track ahead: this takes you past the old stone barns at Dick's Old Walls and on to Swinhoe Farm.

4 Close to Swinhow Farm, go through a gate (often left open), then turn left through another gate to follow a wide stone track signed 'Public Footpath: Holburn 3½ Fenwick 4'. This track passes Swinhoe Lake on your right and then winds its way through Virgin Hill Wood.

D The track down from Dick's Old Walls to Swinhoe Farm is bordered on its left side by a long straight hedge composed almost entirely of hawthorn. Many such hedges were planted following the Enclosure Acts of the 18th and 19th centuries when areas of common land were divided up into small family-sized fields. At this time, hawthorn was a popular shrub for hedging because it was cheap, the spines deter livestock and it grows quickly (hence its alternative name of 'quickthorn'). This hedge makes an interesting contrast to the hedge on the left of the track just past Swinhoe Farm. As a general rule of thumb hedges can be aged by counting the number of different shrub and tree species in a thirty metre stretch, with one species for every 100 years of age. The first 30 metres of hedge past the gate at Swinhoe has six species (hornbeam, rose, elder, beech, holly and hawthorn) which means that it could be as much as 600 years old - possibly taking its origins back to the time of Henry V and the Battle of Agincourt. The importance of such old hedges is not only that they are part of our local heritage, but they are also valuable habitats for wildlife, especially in winter when the variety of shrubs provides food and shelter for many insects and birds.

5 At the end of Virgin Hill Wood go through a gate and continue along the track below the gorse covered crags of Fawcett Hill.

6 Past Fawcett Hill the track comes to a gate. Just before the gate, turn back sharp left along a grass path rising gently uphill (signed 'Public Bridleway: St Cuthbert's Cave 1'). Over the brow of the hill, the path takes you through a gate and down towards a pair of wicket gates at a small timber bridge over a stream.

Swinhoe Lake

E The red squirrel is one Britain's best loved wild animals but is now seldom seen in England outside of a few remaining strongholds, most notably around Poole and the Isle of Wight, Thetford Forest in East Anglia, and here in the north - Virgin Hill Wood is one place where you can still see them. Throughout most of England, the red squirrel has been replaced by the grey, a native of North America that was deliberately introduced in the latter half of the 19th century. They spread rapidly and, being larger and more aggressive than the reds, have progressively displaced them across great swathes of the English countryside. The story is less gloomy in Scotland where the greys have been less successful, probably because they prefer broadleaved woodland whilst the reds are better adapted to conifer forests.

© R.Thornton

Another emerging problem is the squirrelpox virus which was spread by grey squirrels imported from North America. Whilst the greys have a natural immunity, the reds do not: those that are infected with the virus often die within just two weeks. Unfortunately, the disease appears to be making its way north of the border and there are concerns that it could have a devastating impact on the Scottish populations, which account for some 75% of all red squirrels in the UK.

© R.Thornton

7 Over the bridge, the path is not very clear but continue in the same direction, going straight up the hill ahead.

8 At the top of the hill, where the path meets with a fence line coming in from the left, go through a wicket gate, then immediately right through a field gate, keeping to the waymarked route of St Cuthbert's Way. Follow this path as it curves to the right around the top corner of a plantation, then heads diagonally downhill. At the junction with the path followed on the outward leg of the walk, turn right and after a few hundred metres turn left over a stile and back down to the car park.

8. Ford Moss and Routin Linn

FROM THE 'MODEL' VILLAGE OF FORD, this walk takes you through the fields and woods of the Ford and Etal Estate to the Ford Moss Nature Reserve. Further on, the cup and ring marked rock at Routin Linn is probably the most impressive example of 'prehistoric rock art' in Northumberland. The return to Ford follows the same route for some of the way, but also takes you on an attractive diversion across the moorlands of Goatscrag Hill and Broom Ridge.

OS Map: *1:25000 Explorer Map 339 (Kelso, Coldstream & Lower Tweed Valley)*
Start: *NU 949376*
Grade: *Moderate: quite a long walk but no strenuous climbs*
Length: *5.9 miles (9.5 km) and about 3½ hours*
Ascent: *170 metres (560 feet): mostly on gentle gradients*

Local services
Heatherslaw Mill, Etal & Milfield
Etal, Milfield & Lowick
Ford, Etal, Milfield & Lowick

Ford Village lies on the banks of the River Till, about 5½ miles to the west of Lowick on the B6353. Ford, and its twin village of Etal, are a popular tourist destination and are well signed off both the A1 and A697. Park in the roadside car park on the eastern edge of the village.

Before starting your walk, it is worth exploring Ford Village: it is very attractive and has a fascinating history, with many of the houses looking as if they are part of a film set for a 19th century period drama.

To start the walk, go to the top of the car park and climb over a stile beside a gate (signed 'Public Footpath: Fordhill ¼') then, after 15 metres, turn left along a narrow path through a wood.

1 On the far side of the wood, go down a few steps and along a path sandwiched between a hedge and a fence. Through a wicket gate, bear half-left across a field, aiming for the left-hand end of the farm cottages at Fordhill in the valley below. (Note: the electricity pole mid-way down this field will be a useful 'marker' for your return leg of the walk – see **9** below.).

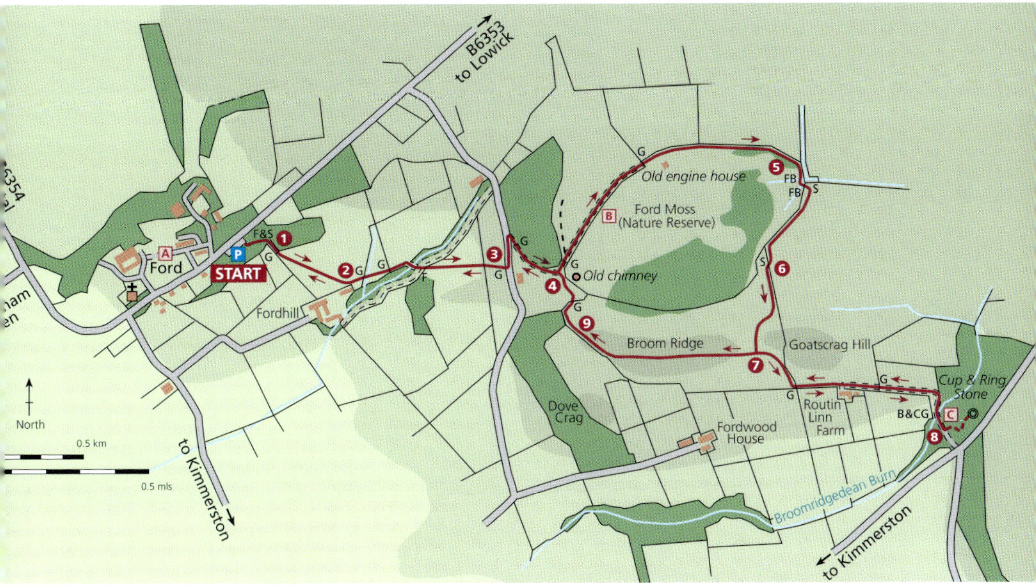

A Ford is a pretty little village set on a hillside overlooking the valley of the River Till. It was created by Louisa, the Marchioness of Waterford (in the south west of Ireland), as a memorial to her husband who suffered a fatal fall from a horse in 1859. It was a major undertaking and she devoted most of the rest of her life to the creation of this 'model' village out of what were then little more than a group of hovels.

The two oldest buildings are Ford Castle and the Church of St Michael and All Angels, both of which are located at the western end of the village. The castle is leased to Northumberland County Council as an outdoor activity centre but, unfortunately, is not open to the public. The church predates the castle, being built in the 13th century, although it was extensively restored in 1853 by John Dobson, a celebrated architect who had a profound impact on the Victorian development of Newcastle. The nave has six mediaeval grave slabs set into the floor, one of which, rather interestingly, is carved with a set of bagpipes - the incumbent must have liked his music.

2 Close to the cottages, turn left along the bottom of the field. After passing through two gates, continue along the field-edge path, then bear right through a gap in a belt of trees to reach a stone farm track. Go over the track and straight across an open field towards a large hawthorn bush in the hedge line ahead (signed 'Public Footpath: Ford Moss ½'). The path continues across the next field to reach a road.

3 Turn left along the road then, after about 150 metres, turn back sharp right along a gated track onto the 'Ford Moss Nature Reserve' (signed 'Public Bridleway: Routing Linn 1¾ Southmoor 2').

4 At the end of the wood, as an old mine chimney comes into view, keep left along the track. (An interpretation panel on a small knoll overlooking the Moss tells you a little about its history, wildlife and management). Through a gate, the track continues along the northern edge of the Moss and past a ruined stone building that was once an engine house for a nearby colliery.

B Ford Moss is a Nature Reserve managed by the Northumberland Wildlife Trust: the term 'moss' is often used in the north of England to describe a peat bog. Over the last 50 years or so this type of wetland habitat has becoming increasingly rare because it was often seen as being unproductive and ripe for improvement, either through drainage to enhance its agricultural value or by planting it with conifer trees to produce timber. Ford Moss is home to a wide variety of plants, insects, birds, mammals and amphibians, some of which are quite rare, and it is now formally designated as a 'Special Area of Conservation' in recognition of its national importance.

Ford Moss is also of historical interest because it is the site of a former colliery that operated from the late 17th century until about 1930. Maps dating from 1860 show a thriving little enterprise with a network of pits and other buildings along the north western edge of the Moss. All that now remain are the old chimney, the floors of some of the old miners' cottages and the shell of the engine house. The mines were quite shallow, but were plagued with water problems because most of the coal seams dipped to the east underneath the Moss. Pumps were installed in an attempt to solve the problem but none worked very well and the colliery eventually had to close.

Ford Moss from the western end of Broom Ridge

5 At the far end of the Moss, ignore the first wicket gate on the left and, 20 metres further on, go over two timber footbridges and a stile. Follow the path to the right which takes you up a gentle hill beside a fence and then a wall.

The solitary Scots pine tree on Broom Ridge

6 Climb the ladder stile over the wall and turn left along a narrow path continuing up the hill – ignoring the wide path going straight on into the trees. As you approach Goatscrag Hill the path veers to the right, away from the wall, to take you over Broom Ridge. On the far side of the ridge, the path meets (at a T-junction) a wider grass path running east-west along the contour.

7 At the path junction, turn left and head towards the rocky crags on Goatscrag Hill, then down to a wicket gate close to the farm fields. (If you want to miss out on this section of the walk to the 'Cup and Ring Marked Rock' at Routin Linn, turn right at the path T-junction and continue from 9). At the bottom of the slope turn left through the wicket gate and on to Routin Linn Farm. Walk along the track to the left of the farm buildings and follow this to the cattle grid bridge over the Broomridgedean Burn.

8 About 50 metres past the bridge, at the top of a rise, turn left along a path into the woods then, 20 metres further on, go right. The path winds its way through the wood, over a couple of very steep little ridges (actually the ramparts of an iron age fort), and then brings you to a clearing with the large cup and ring marked rock in the centre – the distance from the farm track to the rock is about 175 metres. From the rock, retrace your steps back to Routin Linn Farm and then to the path junction at Point 7: here, just keep straight on along the wide path heading west along Broom Ridge.

C Routin Linn is the site of one of the most impressive 'cup and ring' marked rocks in Northumberland. This type of prehistoric 'rock art' dates from the Bronze Age (2100 – 700 BC) or even earlier, and is widespread across northern England and southern Scotland where there is soft sandstone rock which is easy to engrave. When you are looking at the rock, please be careful not to stand or walk on the markings - they have been here for about 4000 years and are an important part of our heritage.

The reason why ancient Britons carved these marks and what they represent is a mystery, although theories include maps of the stars, representations of settlements or records of ownership. This also raises the question of whether they were purely artistic, with no specific meaning, or had some deeper religious or cultural significance. Recent research has also drawn parallels with the types of rock carving still used by some native American societies where they are seen as messages from their ancestors, possibly symbolising the link between life on earth and an afterlife. Whatever their meaning, the motivation for carving them must have died out in the middle of the Bronze Age (about 1500BC) because none have been found that can be dated to a later period.

9 At the far end of Broom Ridge, go past a solitary pine tree on the skyline and continue downhill along a path beside a stone wall. At the bottom of the hill, go through a wicket gate and back to the track close to the old mine chimney. From here, retrace the route taken on the outward leg of your walk back to the car park in Ford Village – the only tricky bit can be finding the path through the field above the cottages at Fordhill, but the electricity pole in the middle of the field gives you a good line.

D When you have finished your walk, it is well worth visiting the nearby site of the Battle of Flodden - one of the most important battles ever fought between England and Scotland. Flodden lies a few miles to the west, close to the village of Branxton. The 'Battlefield Trail' is excellent and includes some informative interpretive panels.

Flodden was the culmination of a conflict between England and Scotland which started when King James IV of Scotland declared war on England to honour the 'Auld Alliance' between Scotland and France. James's aim was to divert the army of Henry VIII from his campaign against the French King Louis XII. Flodden has been called Britain's last great mediaeval battle because it was fought with weapons that had been used for centuries but which, with the advent of artillery, were becoming obsolete. The Scots relied on the pike (a long thrusting spear that was used two-handed) whilst the English used the bill (a bill-hook with a long handle and spike at the end). The pike was not suited to close quarter fighting, especially on the uneven and boggy ground where the main engagement took place: this put the Scots at a big disadvantage and played a major part in their defeat.

The loss of so many Scottish lives at Flodden is commemorated in the lament, *The Floo'ers o' the Forest*, which describes the grief of wives and mothers at the death of their young men: the first few lines go as follows (although you may need a Scot to translate):

I've heard the lilting, at the yowe-milking,
Lassies a-lilting before dawn o' day;
But now they are moaning on ilka green loaning;
The Flooers o' the Forest are a' wede away.

Dool and wae for the order sent oor lads tae the Border!
The English for ance, by guile wan the day,
The Flooers o' the Forest, that fought aye the foremost,
The pride o' oor land lie cauld in the clay.

Goatscrag Hill from the Broom Ridge path

9. Around Holy Island

BEFORE EXPLORING THE REMOTER PARTS OF HOLY ISLAND, this walk takes you past the more popular sights, including the ruins of the priory, the old harbour and the castle. From here, the walk heads off the tourist trail along the island's eastern and northern shores, with its wetlands and reedbeds, deserted beaches and rocky headlands and, on warmer days, the chance to see seals basking on rocks along the shoreline.

OS Map: *1:25000 Explorer Map 340 (Holy Island and Bamburgh)*
Start: *NU 126424*
Grade: *Easy - although the walk is quite long*
Length: *5.3 miles (8.5 km) and about 3 hours*
Ascent: *Minimal*

Local services
- Beal & Holy Island Village
- Holy Island Village & West Mains (A1 junction)
- Holy Island Village

Holy Island is accessed via a causeway and is cut off at high tide. Before visiting, check the tide tables at **www.lindisfarne.org.uk** and make sure you have enough time to complete the walk.

The walk starts from the island's main car park on the left side of the road as you enter the village from the causeway.

From the car park, turn left along the main road, past the Lindisfarne Hotel, towards the centre of the village. At the T-junction, turn right, then take an immediate left down the road signed to Lindisfarne Priory and the Priory Museum. At the market cross, keep straight on, following the sign to the Priory: the Lindisfarne Priory Museum is on the right.

Lindisfarne Priory

1. Past the Museum, go through the gate into St Mary's churchyard, then bear right along the path between the gravestones and make for the gateway in the churchyard wall, then turn left and follow the winding track towards the sea. Near the bottom of the hill, as the track curves to the right, turn left onto a grassy shelf and follow the path left up a stony bank to the top of The Heugh.

2. Walk past the coastguard lookout and the war memorial, then follow the path left down to a group of fishery sheds. Bear left along a wide track with 'The Ouse' (the little harbour) to your right. The track meets a road as it makes its way eastwards from the village. Turn right along the road, towards the castle.

A In the days when sailing ships plied the seas around Great Britain, the offshore reefs and small islands along the Northumberland coast took a heavy toll, especially amongst the smaller trawlers and merchantmen. The harbour on Lindisfarne was a place of refuge from North Sea gales and storms and will have saved the lives of many sailors.

In the early years of the 19th century Trinity House commissioned the construction of the two navigation beacons that can be seen over on the mainland to the south west. When they were lined up, they provided sailors with the correct bearing for their approach to the deep channel that led to the harbour. Known as East Old Law and West Old Law they are about 25 metres high and were built in the shape of elongated pyramids and originally had an iron triangle on a metal staff on top. With the changing currents, which altered the channels in the approach to the island harbour, the bearing of the beacons can no longer be relied upon.

Further along your walk you will come to a large white granite obelisk on Emmanuel Head which was also built by Trinity House at about the same time. Over the years, many sailing ships had come to grief on the rocks around Emmanuel Head because they mistook this headland for Castle Point to the south, which marked the northern entrance to the harbour. This white granite pyramid was therefore constructed as a 'daymark beacon' to distinguish it from Castle Point and warn sailors to keep well clear.

3 Go through the gate at the end of the road and follow the cobbled track to the right of the castle. At the castle entrance, keep straight ahead past the upturned boats (one of which houses an interpretive display about their history) and to the left of a rocky knoll. The path soon drops down to cross a timber footbridge: before doing so, take a few minutes to have a look at the lime kilns to your right. From the footbridge, continue along the raised tramway as it curves to the left.

'The Lough' and a reed bunting, one of its commoner residents

4 Go through a pair of gates above the rocks at Scar Jockey and then follow the grass track heading northwards for several hundred metres, keeping a wall/fence close by on your left. This takes you to the open water and marshland of 'The Lough'.

B Lindisfarne Castle (photograph left) must be one of the most picturesque, and most photographed, sites in northern England, making frequent appearances on anything from biscuit tins and calendars to TV commercials and films - in the last case, perhaps most famously, in Roman Polanski's typically sombre 1971 version of Shakespeare's Macbeth, where it doubled for Glamis Castle.

The castle sits on a small whinstone crag called Beblowe Hill and was built in the 1550s using stone from Lindisfarne Priory which had been demolished on the orders of Henry VIII. During the reign of Elizabeth I the castle walls were strengthened and platforms were built for the cannons that protected the nearby harbour. In 1901 it became the property of Edward Hudson, the owner of Country Life magazine, who had it restored in the 'Arts and Crafts' style by Sir Edward Lutyens. The walled garden to the north of the castle, originally the garrison's vegetable plot, was designed by Lutyen's friend, the celebrated garden designer Gertrude Jekyll. The castle and garden are now owned by the National Trust and both are open to visitors at certain times of year (see **www.nationaltrust.org.uk** for details).

5 20 metres past the bird-hide at The Lough, take the path to the right heading back towards the sea: this soon re-joins the shoreline path running north along the coast. Go through a wicket gate and then, a few hundred metres further on, climb over a stile to enter the Lindisfarne National Nature Reserve: the white obelisk on Emmanuel Head lies straight ahead.

6 From Emmanuel Head, follow a dune path around the curve of Sandham Bay to the headland at Nessend or, if the tide is out, drop down onto the beach.

7 Past Nessend, the path runs along the top of some high and precipitous cliffs: take great care to keep away from the edge and keep a watchful eye on children and dogs. The route around Coves Haven to Snipe Point follows a well defined grass path along the back of the main dune ridge: again, an alternative option, if the tide is out, is to walk along the beach.

8 Beyond Snipe Point, the path keeps to the dune ridge above the rocky shoreline.

C The rocks that lie just offshore along this section of coast are a popular spot for grey seals to bask on warmer days between spring and autumn. You will often hear them before you see them: their cries have an ethereal and haunting quality which, with a bit of imagination, perhaps gives a clue to the origin of Celtic myths about seals being mistaken for mermaids and luring sailors onto the rocks with their enchanting songs.

Grey seals are one of the rarest seals in the world with about 40% of the total population living in the seas around Great Britain. They spend most the year at sea but come ashore in the autumn to form breeding colonies on rocky shores and beaches, often preferring uninhabitated islands where they will be free from disturbance. This part of the Northumberland coast is home to about 3000 – 4000 grey seals, with about 1000 pups being born each year. Commercial hunting and large scale culling came to an end in the late 1970s and since that time the UK population has increased significantly. The Farne Islands, just to the south of Holy Island, are a popular spot and the boat trips from Seahouses harbour will give you an opportunity to see them - and lots of other wildlife - at close quarters.

© M Byron

Cowslips and early purple orchids on the Holy Island dunes

D The National Nature Reserve at Lindisfarne is one of the largest in the UK, taking in over 15 miles of coastline from the Tweed Estuary to Budle Bay and including most of Holy Island. The importance of this area for wildlife stems from the richness and diversity of the different habitats, which include extensive areas of sand dunes, saltmarshes and mudflats. The dune slacks (i.e. the damper hollows) on Holy Island are especially colourful in spring and early summer when there are impressive shows of cowslips, bloody cranesbills, marsh orchids and marsh helleborines. Autumn and winter are the best time for birds, with six internationally important species of wildfowl and waders overwintering here, having flown in from northern Europe and Russia to take advantage of the milder winters and the abundant food that can be found in the inter-tidal mudflats. Of particular importance are the pale-bellied brent geese, pinkfooted and greylag geese, wigeon, grey plovers and bar-tailed godwits.

9 Around a headland, where the rocks on the shoreline come to an end, look for a gap in a fence line on the dune ridge just above the beach: from here, head inland along the grass path that runs to the left side of a high knoll about 100 metres away. On the far side of the knoll, the path bears slightly right to another dune ridge about 200 yards further on: over this ridge, the distant skyline of Holy Island village comes into view ahead. The path soon becomes a wide and very distinct grass track, with the prominent outline of the village water tower providing a useful direction guide.

10 On reaching the road, go through the wicket gate and turn left to get back to the car park.

10. Norham Castle and the Tweed Riverside

NORHAM IS A QUIET LITTLE VILLAGE where life, and the River Tweed, slide past at a tranquil pace. The starting point for the walk is Norham Castle, which was built during more turbulent times when England was seen by the Scots on the other side of the river, as the 'auld enemy'. The first half of the walk heads upstream along the banks of the Tweed, a river famous for its salmon fishing, before turning east along the wooded valley of Newbiggin Dean. The final section follows a road for part of the way, then cuts through woodlands and pastures back to Norham.

OS Map: *1:25000 Explorer Map 339 (Kelso, Coldstream & Lower Tweed Valley)*
Start: *NT 907475*
Grade: *Easy*
Length: *4.0 miles (6.5 km) and about 2½ hours*
Ascent: *Minimal*

Local services
- Norham, Horncliffe
- Norham, Horncliffe
- Norham

Park in the English Heritage car park at Norham Castle on the east side of the village on the road linking Norham and Horncliffe. The castle is open from 1st April to 30th September (10.00am – 5.00pm) on Saturdays, Sundays and Bank Holidays. If the Castle and car park are closed, park on the grass verge close to the entrance.

Walk back through the car park and past the entrance, then across the grass to an old stone archway that leads into the main part of the castle. Leave the castle via the timber bridge over the moat, then go through the entrance gate and walk along the roadside pavement into the village. If the castle and car park are closed and you park on the verge, walk along the pavement into Norham village rather than through the grounds – you still get a very good view of the castle.

Norham Castle

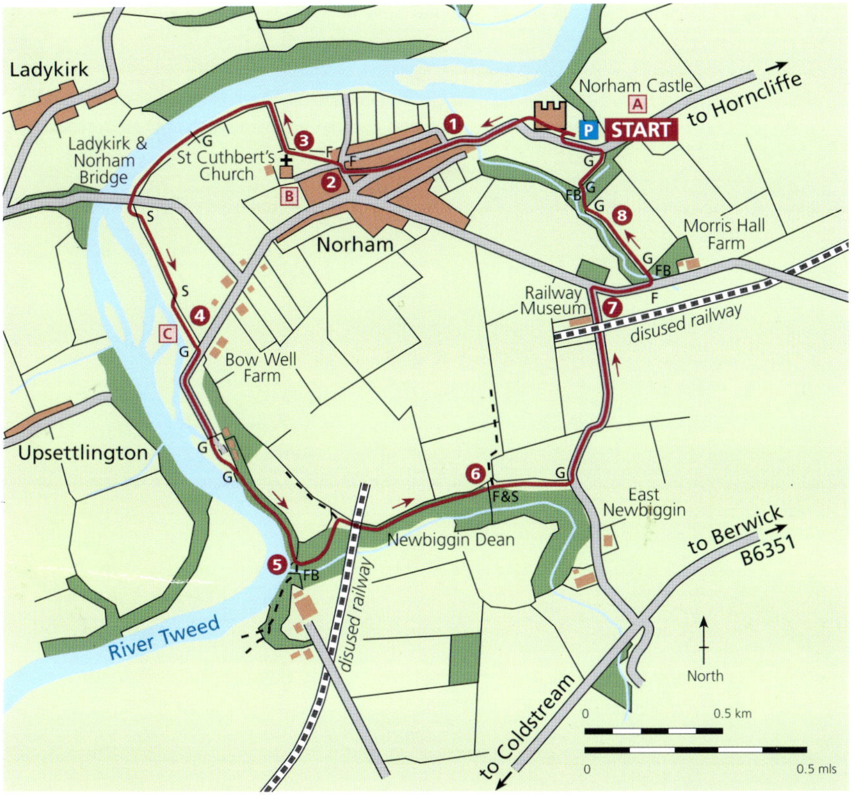

A Norham Castle (photograph left) was first built by Bishop Ranulph Flambard of Durham in 1121 with the aim of protecting his lands from 'robbers and Scots' and controlling a vital ford over the River Tweed. The original castle probably covered much the same area as today, with the main defensive structure being a stone 'great hall' which would have been surrounded by a timber palisade and ditch.

Norham was one of the strongest, and most frequently attacked, of the border castles. Records suggest that it was besieged at least 13 times by the Scots - once for nearly a year by Robert Bruce - and it was called 'the most dangerous and adventurous place in the country'. Unfortunately, even its powerful 12th-century keep and massive towered bailey walls could not resist the heavy cannon of the Scottish King James IV, and it fell to him in 1513. Shortly afterwards, the tables were turned on James when he suffered a catastrophic defeat at nearby Flodden at the hands of an English army under the command of the Earl of Surrey. King James died at Flodden, along with about 10,000 of his men and much of Scotland's nobility. The battle site lies a few miles to the south of here, close to the village of Branxton and is well worth a visit (see box D on page 53).

1 Continue down the main street (Castle Street) and, close to the Victoria Hotel, keep to the right side of the village green. At the end of the green, turn right towards the war memorial (signed on the corner of the green 'Public Footpath: Ladykirk Bridge ¾ Twizell Bridge 5½').

2 Go through the entrance to St Cuthbert's Parish Church (signed 'Public Footpath: River Tweed ¼') and bear half-right along the grass path between the gravestones.

B St Cuthbert's is a rather attractive church, albeit in a rather squat and solid way: it was designed by the same architect as Norham Castle and it looks as though he was still in 'castles mode' when he produced the blueprint for the church.

The first church at Norham was founded in about 830AD. The coffin of St Cuthbert was brought here for safe keeping in 875 AD when Danish invaders destroyed the priory at Lindisfarne where he had been buried some 200 years earlier. The present church was started in 1165 and, over the succeeding centuries, has been rebuilt and extended on several occasions. It was here in 1292 that John Balliol did homage to King Edward I of England (the 'Hammer of the Scots' of 'Braveheart' fame) after he had been chosen as King of Scotland. Nearly 30 years later Robert Bruce occupied and fortified the church during his year-long failed attempt to seize Norham Castle from the English. The church has now settled to a far quieter existence and visitors are welcome to look around: leaflets are available inside the entrance for those who want to know more about its history and architecture.

3 At the end of the graveyard, turn right through a gap in a wall and down a narrow path between two hedges: this takes you to the river, where you should turn left and head upstream along the banks of the River Tweed. The path takes you under the Ladykirk and Norham Bridge, then bears left to a stile in a fence. Over the stile, turn right and follow the path along the edge of a field: this takes you to another stile then continues through the riverside woodlands.

Ladykirk and Norham Bridge

4 Go through a wicket gate at the end of the wood and turn right along a tarmac road. As the road becomes a stone track, bear right through a wicket gate and across the riverside grassland (in summer – a nice spot for a picnic). At the end of the field, go through a gate and follow a path through a wood.

5 About 20 metres before reaching a concrete footbridge over a stream the path divides: here, take the left fork along the path heading away from the River Tweed (i.e. not over the footbridge). Another 130 metres further on, bear left up some stone steps. At the top of the slope, turn right at the path T-junction: this takes you through a stone archway (under an old railway line) and onto a path along the top of Newbiggin Dean.

6 Go over a stile beside a gate, then continue along the path above the Dean (signed 'Public Footpath; East Newbiggin ¼'), ignoring the path over the fields to the left. At the road - taking care at all times to watch and listen for oncoming traffic - cross over onto the far side, turn left and walk along the verge.

7 At the T Junction, turn right and continue along the verge on the right-hand side of the road. About 50 metres past the start of a wood on the left side of the road, cross the road - again taking care - and take the path to the left signed 'Public Bridleway: Norham Castle ½'. Go over a timber footbridge and through a wicket gate, then follow the grass path along the left side of the field.

The River Tweed near Norham

C The Tweed is one of the best salmon rivers in Europe and draws fishermen from all over the world. At Norham, the Tweed forms the border between Scotland and England, but it is commonly regarded as a Scottish river because most of its 96 mile length lies in Scotland.

Atlantic salmon begin their life in the upper reaches of the river where the female lays her eggs in the gravel. Depending on the water temperature and availability of food, the young salmon will spend from one to five years in the river before heading out into the north Atlantic, often to the waters off Greenland and Norway. They usually stay in the ocean for two or three years before returning to their native river to breed: it is during this 'run' up the river that most are caught. About 90-95% of all Atlantic salmon die following their first breeding season but some females do survive to spawn two, or even three times, with these survivors returning to the sea to feed between spawnings.

Fly fishing is the commonest and most exciting way to catch salmon. Rods are 4 - 5 metres in length and the flies go by such colourful names as 'Munroe's Killer', 'Stoat's Tail' and 'Thunder and Lightning'. Sizes of fish vary from about 4lb up to about 20lb, and occasionally as much as 30lb: the salmon in the photograph weighed about 8lb and was caught in a pool under the Ladykirk and Norham Bridge.

8 A wicket gate in the corner of the field leads to a path through a wood: on the far side go over a footbridge and through a wicket gate, then turn right along the field edge to a roadside gate. Through the gate, turn left, back to the car park.